WINTER BIRDS
of the Carolinas and Nearby States

WINTER BIRDS

of the Carolinas and Nearby States

BY MICHAEL A. GODFREY

JOHN F. BLAIR, *Publisher*
Winston-Salem, North Carolina

Library of Congress Cataloging in Publication Data

Godfrey, Michael A   1940–
    Winter birds of the Carolinas and nearby states.
    Includes index.

    1. Birds—North Carolina   2.   Birds—South Carolina.
3.   Birds—United States.   I.   Title.
QL684.N8G6   598.2'9756   76–56988
ISBN 0–910244–94–4

cedar waxwing

red-shouldered hawk

For Janet

Acknowledgments

Some who live and work with nature are loners, but I don't see how they manage. In photographing these birds and writing this book about them, I drew heavily on the strength, love, knowledge and generosity of others. Their contributions made *Winter Birds* possible. So it should be, I think, for experiences with the natural world—even those so personal as to be considered mystic—are better when shared.

Janet Stephens shared the days and nights of research and writing, then typed and pre-edited the manuscript, so my greatest debt is to her. Stanley Alford led me through miles of the Carolina countryside so that I could photograph the birds, and he took several of the pictures himself when I failed. Angelo Caparella saved me miles of legwork in the UNC Zoology Library. Both Stanley and Angelo were generous with their field notes. Bob and Liz Teulings fielded many a technical inquiry, and Helmut Mueller endured his share concerning the raptors. Bill Clark of the Cape May Bird Observatory gave me access to his breath-taking world of accipiters and falcons; his organization deserves the support of all who love the birds of prey. The staff at the Hawk Mountain Sanctuary was notably helpful. Louise and Bill Stickel of the Patuxent Wildlife Research Center, who were instrumental in identifying DDT as the scourge of our raptors, provided perspective on the problems these birds face. Duane Raver, editor of *Wildlife in North Carolina*, was supportive in many ways. I am grateful to George Scheer, my literary agent and overall counselor on this project. And for sharing their sacred farmlands with me, I am especially thankful to Bob and Dot Hogan, Bob and Martha Kirk, Broughton and Grace Copelan, and Bob Nutter.

Finally, I decry the tradition of failing to acknowledge the hard work and personal involvement of publisher and editor. John F. Blair and Rick Mashburn organized and polished the material in this book, and I am grateful to them.

Contents

Foreword

A Philosophy of Observation

The uplands of the Carolinas and nearby states constitute a life system. Micro-ecologists would say it is composed of many smaller systems; those of a more holistic view might see the region functioning as a mere subsystem of a global supersystem. The traditional American Indian view is that the earth is a single organism of which every creature is an integral part; hence, to harm the earth is to harm one's self and, conversely, one can not engage in self abuse without harming the earth. The views of the ferment of life are many and are personal to each human—to each creature, for all we know. At any rate, it is no longer practical to look upon man apart from nature. Humans live in and are sustained by a life system of some dimension, and that is a fact that no amount of pavement, plastic and suburbanism can obscure. Similarly, the lives of other creatures can be comprehended only in the context of their surroundings.

Like any life system, that of our region is composed of autotrophic organisms, or producers, which take their energy directly from the sun, and heterotrophic organisms, or consumers, which are sustained by eating autotrophs and other heterotrophs. Green plants and algae are the autotrophs. They capture solar energy and fix in it their tissue in combination with minerals from the soil. The green plant tissue is ingested by primary heterotrophs, such as insects, fungi and cattle. The primary heterotrophs yield their energy and nutrients to secondary consumers including birds, bacteria and people.

The simplicity of this model is shattered in actuality by convoluted consumption cycles more closely akin to four-dimensional labyrinths, time included, than to the more comprehensible "food chain" analogies often used for illustration. Birds and people are secondary heterotrophs only when eating primary consumers such as insects and cattle. But not only do birds eat insects, but insects eat birds. They also eat people, before and after we die. And birds eat berries whose seeds pass to the soil, prepared, in some cases, to germinate only because they passed through an avian digestive tract. The resulting plants later become food for deer and cattle, whose droppings are picked over in winter by grackles, who eat horn worms off people's tomato plants the following summer.

The realization that these complex interrelationships exist is a recent development in scientific circles, possibly less recent among those who have traditionally lived close to the soil. We find that the ties between organisms are not just extensive; they are endless. To attempt to comprehend them fully is an exercise in vanity. Perhaps it is adequate just to be aware of their existence, to acknowledge that the humans of our region and the other animals and plants are not just here, but are here *because* of one another.

The popular term for a person who looks at birds or trees or butterflies as participants in a life system is *naturalist*. The naturalist acknowledges the system, however sketchily he comprehends it, and views himself as part of the system. *Winter Birds of the Carolinas and Nearby States* is written for the naturalist.

Providing a means to recognize the birds of our region, of our life system, is a minor objective of the book. Its more important contribution is to offer a glimpse of the birds' life styles and to suggest how they contribute to the flow of energy and nutrients that sustains the observer and the observed. The objective is to set into motion a process of thought and style of observation that the citizen-naturalist can use to develop his own concept of our region's life scheme, himself included.

A Method of Observation

Accustomed to thinking in terms of habitats and life systems, the naturalist tunes his senses to the locality and is ever watchful. Though others may be oblivious to them, the sights and sounds of nature enrich the daily routine of the naturalist: the buzz of a nighthawk picked from among the noises of city traffic on a summer evening, the hush that comes over a yardful of birds at the approach of a sharp-shinned hawk. Even when the naturalist visits beyond familiar landmarks, his basic understanding of interrelationships yields discoveries.

A computer expert from Florida who was very much interested in birds visited my office in Chapel Hill one June morning. As we talked about his product, a mockingbird outside the window prattled its usual mimicry of real and imagined sounds. Finally the computer man asked if a lot of evening grosbeaks had wintered in the vicinity. Twice in half an hour he had heard the mockingbird give the grosbeak's chimed notes and had surmised, correctly, that the grosbeaks had given the mockingbird an earful the previous winter.

Alert, sensitive persons who are attuned to the world around them have limitless opportunities to see and identify the birds and to observe their ecology. Such persons become aware that even in modern times and in highly civilized places the birdlife has struck a balance with the other elements of the local life scheme, man-made and natural. The community lives on, to the benefit of some bird species, to the detriment of others.

Thus, the first specific suggestion on how to observe birds is to be always receptive. Don't look at the sidewalk; look at the shrubs and trees around you as you walk. Don't let the noise of traffic or the conversation of people around you mask the sounds of birds. The sounds are present almost everywhere, almost all the time. It is simply a question of attentiveness of the same kind that a mother applies to the cry of her infant in the next room; it will be heard regardless of the ambient noise. Training the eyes and ears, more specifically increasing the receptiveness of the brain, is the basis for embarking on an alternative awareness—that of the naturalist to the life system in which he participates.

Concentrate on form and movement. Learn the birds' perched and in-flight silhouettes. Know the profile of the flight path, the regularity and frequency of the wingbeat, the depth of the wing stroke, the dihedral angle of the wings during soaring or gliding flight. Each bird, or at least each family of birds, has a unique set of flight characteristics, a distinctive shape when perched. The rounded tail of the Cooper's hawk distinguishes it from the square-tailed sharp-shin. The mockingbird's deep rowing wingbeats are markedly different from the loggerhead shrike's rapid shallow strokes, though the two birds are of similar size and color.

Do *not* concentrate on color. Many distantly related birds wear similar colors, such as the slate blue that adorns the backs of the white-breasted nuthatch, the great blue heron and the belted kingfisher, although each is in a different order. The colors of some birds change so drastically with the seasons that early observers thought that the spring and winter plumages cloaked different species. The American goldfinch is an example. The colors of some young birds, such as robins, differ significantly from adult plumages. Perhaps the most important reason to avoid a primary reliance on color for identifying birds is that colors are not always visible. I would go so far as to say that they are *usually* not visible. The majority of sightings are at a distance or against a background that makes the detection of color unreliable or impossible. Against an overcast sky, for example, most birds appear dark and colorless. Form and movement, not color, must provide the primary clues for identification.

I do not mean to say that color is without significance. Color becomes useful when a detailed view can be had, perhaps through field glasses, and when the markings and nuances of color can help distinguish between closely similar species.

Watch for birds as you travel. Birds of prey stand starkly silhouetted against the sky when perched in dead snags near the road. If time permits and you've brought your field glasses, you can stop and watch, at a respectful distance, and probably see the predator in action as it swoops from its hunting perch to make a kill. From your car you'll see many birds in flight: vultures soaring high, woodpeckers flying fast and direct with deep undulations.

Roadside utility wires provide unobstructed views of the ground below, and many species use them as hunting and resting perches. Even the smallest birds stand out conspicuously against the sky when they rest on wires. In a fraction of a second you can scan the wires ahead and see birds at a considerable distance without diverting attention from your driving. Here again, form is important. The sparrow hawk and the mourning dove are frequent users of roadside wires, and they are approximately equal in size; but you can distinguish the two a quarter-mile away by the little falcon's larger head. The bluebird's hunched posture differentiates it from numerous other small birds who perch on the wires. And occasionally the top two feet of a utility pole spreads long, broad wings and flaps

away in the form of a red-tailed hawk or a great horned owl. With training, your eyes pounce on any irregularity in the roadside utility wires, poles and cross members to yield a rich assortment of bird sightings and to enliven what might otherwise be a tedious road trip. Even traveling at unnatural speeds and separated from the natural world by metal and glass, you can still deepen your rapport with the sustaining life forces as the miles pass.

Learn all the bird sounds you can. The task seems overwhelming at first, no less formidable than learning another language. But as the mind becomes receptive to nature, bird sounds are among the more strident stimuli to reach out to us. The ability to identify birds, if only a few species, by sound greatly enlarges our awareness of nature, for we hear much more often than we see. In winter, birds are less vocal than in other seasons, and the number of calls is much more manageable than at the height of the nesting season, when territorial pronouncements resound.

Taking a walk with someone experienced with birdcalls is one way to learn. Another method is to memorize a call, then find it on a birdcall recording, several of which are commercially available. Such recordings are effective learning aids, but their use can be frustrating in that by the time you have listened to several closely similar calls you may forget the one to be identified.

The most effective method is to *see* the bird give its call. The visual and aural association of a bird opening its mouth to sing is not quickly forgotten, especially if preceded by a difficult stalk through briars or by a number of frustrating failures.

Be mindful of habit and habitat. Is it an open field, and is the hawk flying just above the grass? A marsh hawk for sure, even before you get to see the white rump spot. Soaring high over the field? A glance at the light underparts will probably confirm that it is a red-tailed hawk. If the same events were observed in a hardwood forest, the raptors would probably be Cooper's and red-shouldered hawks, respectively. "I know it was a woodpecker," a friend tells you, "but it was on the ground. Then it flew up to a tree and perched *across* a limb, not against the trunk, as woodpeckers usually do." You don't have to ask if the bird was brown with a black bib, a white rump and a red chevron at the back of its head. The common flicker is the only woodpecker in our region whose behavior fits that description.

In summary, a naturalist's manner of observation is to note form and action, consider the place of observation, and be always receptive.

Introduction

Winter intensifies the relationships between birds and humans. Many species forage closer to human habitations then as purely wild food supplies dwindle. Some freely enter our dooryards to glean our wasted or planted foods or to accept the food we intentionally provide for them. Others remain wary and keep to the fields, marshes and woodlands, but because of the seasonal defoliation, they are more readily sighted.

The wintering bird population in the uplands of the Carolinas and nearby states is composed of a predictable set of species. After the warm-weather birds who nested with us emigrate southward and after the northern migrants traverse the region on their way to the tropics, the region is left with its corps of wintering stalwarts. Our wintering birds include many who have arrived from the north and about twice that number who share with us the fortunes of all seasons but who come into our awareness most strongly in winter. Birds such as the chickadees, the titmice and even the vocal and flashy cardinals retire into the foliage during the nesting season. They concentrate then on insects for their own nourishment and for that of their insatiably hungry young. Autumn reduces the availability of insects and presents the birds with a sequence of ripening fruits and seeds. By winter the birds' diet has shifted almost entirely to seeds and to the persisting fruit of a few important plants, including dogwood, poke, black gum and honeysuckle. Those birds anatomically unsuited to making this dietary shift move southward in pursuit of flying insects or flowers or whatever their speciality may be. The constant search for ever-dwindling food supplies obliges the remaining birds to exploit every opportunity for feeding, even if that brings them into contact with humans.

Emboldened by hunger, birds in winter become much more a force in our lives than in the warmer months when food is no problem for them.

A few of the species that might be seen in our region in winter are casual visitors whose sporadic presence does not justify inclusion.

The Carolinas and nearby states, from southern Pennsylvania to northern Georgia, host approximately common wintering bird populations in physiographically comparable locations throughout the region. With minor changes, the wintering birdlife in the Appalachians is constant from Pennsylvania southward, and the birds found in cities along the fall line from Philadelphia to Atlanta differ by only a few species.

As we proceed northward through the eastern seaboard states, the mountains edge closer to the sea, constricting the width of the Piedmont and Coastal Plain physiographic provinces. The increasing proximity of the sea moderates the climate and roughly compensates for the change in latitude. Therefore some species of birds are as comfortable wintering for example near Wilmington, Delaware, as in the vicinity of Charleston, South Carolina, and, not surprisingly, find comparable habitats in widely distant sections of the region.

Drawing lines on a map to delineate the boundaries of the region encompassed by "the Carolinas and Nearby States" is judgmental, if not arbitrary. We can say, however, that an observer proceeding northward from a central point in the region, say Raleigh, North Carolina, would find that somewhere northwest of Philadelphia the climate began to thin the ranks of soft-billed birds such as those in the thrush, thrasher, wren and kinglet families and to add some of the more boreal species including crossbills and snow buntings. Proceeding southward from the same starting point, the observer would see the wintering birdlife change significantly as he approached the Gulf coast and the southern Atlantic coast. He would logically draw the southern boundary of the region to exclude Florida and the southern thirds of Georgia, Alabama and Mississippi. The Mississippi and Ohio rivers suggest convenient westward limits because the climatic and physiographic continuity of the eastern deciduous forests *very* roughly observes these boundaries. However, a large percentage, even a majority, of the birds within the region winter on both sides of this vast drainage system.

No logic associates political borders with the rhythms of the birds' lives. Substitute the black-capped for the Carolina chickadee, deduct a few warblers, and you have converted the wintering birds of the Carolinas to those of Maryland. Other slight changes expand the region's boundaries southward and westward of the Carolinas. Where gross changes occur, the region defined as "the Carolinas and Nearby States" reaches its ornithological limits.

"Winter" and "Carolinas and Nearby States" define the seasonal and geographic limits to the scope of this book. An additional limitation is the exclusion of birds whose habitats are confined to coastal aquatic locations and who are not found inland of the effects of the tides. Specifically excluded are all swimming birds: ducks, geese, swans, loons, grebes and coots. These limits allow focus on 88 of the more than 350 species recorded in the eastern United States.

Arrangement of This Book

The birds included in this book are divided into four groups to facilitate recognition.

"At the Feeder" includes those birds who in my ex-
perience are likely to respond to some sort of food offering in winter. Some of these may not eat directly at a feeding station but prefer to forage for food tossed to the ground by other birds. Birds, such as the brown thrasher and golden-crowned kinglet, who are occasionally attracted into a feeding area by the apparent safety and prosperity of others but who do not eat the food offered by humans are not included in this section. Not all birds eat seed or bread crumbs; some prefer suet or table scraps or a mixture of cornmeal, peanut butter and bacon fat. Any feeding situation will draw more birds if a birdbath is provided to complement the meal, but those who come in only for a bath are not included in this section. I hasten to add that my experience in the matter is not complete and that others may know of instances where some of the birds I have placed in other sections habitually accept human offerings. It is probable, however, that any bird you see at your feeder will be found in this section.

"Farther Afield" encompasses the birds of the region, other than the rare and uncommon species and the raptors, who are unlikely to visit a feeder. The birds who accept food from people, and are therefore listed in the previous section, are also seen afield, of course. Many birds in this section have close relatives in the first, and their instinct to avoid humans probably reflects no more than a preference for a habitat remote from human traffic. Others belong to families and orders no members of which are characteristically tolerant of humans. If there is "misanthropy" in this attitude, it is in some cases, such as that of the herons and egrets, based on a history of bad experience with man. A less obvious reason for the intolerance of some species toward humans is explored later under "Nomenclature and Taxonomy."

"Birds of Prey" covers the more common raptorial birds wintering in the region. This section includes vultures and shrikes in addition to the hawks and owls likely to be seen (or heard). The birds in this section are, for the most part, large. They are solitary in winter, spending the majority of their time on exposed hunting perches or searching in flight for prey. They are wary and studiously avoid contact with humans.

"Rare and Uncommon Birds" are grouped together for special emphasis. The sighting of any bird in this section is a noteworthy event for the naturalist and should be shared with others.

The material on each bird includes a photograph, some descriptive data to aid in locating and identifying the species, and a natural history profile explaining how the bird fits into the winter life scheme of its chosen habitat.

The photographs were selected from among literally thousands taken by the author and other contributing photographers. Those used were chosen because they best portray the birds' diagnostic features, although they may not have been the most "beautiful" of the photographs reviewed. All portray their subjects as they appear during winter.

The difficulties in taking good descriptive photographs are worth mentioning, for they reflect some of the obstacles to making field observations. Plumages vary, shadows and objects block the view, constant motion impedes observation. Any number of obstructions can conspire to reduce the usefulness of a photograph as an aid in identification. The artist can depict a bird in any pose and can emphasize the field marks through a variety of means, but the photographer gets only what the birds and conditions offer. Photographing birds in their winter condition deprives the photographer of one of his primary advantages—he can not use a nesting situation to lure the adults into focus.

Nevertheless, I have compiled this descriptive collection, taking the majority of photographs myself and relying on the patience and excellence of other photographers for several important portraits. Some species of birds are by nature unconcerned about the photographer's presence; others can be notably uncooperative. To those who posed with minimal dissent, I am thankful, for their willingness made the project manageable. To those of moderate shyness, I am grateful for the challenge. To those who carried their wariness to extremes, I owe at least six years of intimacy with the outdoors.

Descriptive data includes a series of elements that give the reader information on the appearance, size, sounds and likely location of each species.

FIELD MARKS are the prominent features of anatomy and plumage by which a bird is recognized in the field. The diagram on the following page is provided for the identification of topographical terms used in this section.

LENGTH of a bird is most useful to the naturalist when it is measured from beak to tail in the posture in which the bird is most likely to be seen. I found that for many birds the figures for body length given in several reference books varied by as much as 25% mostly because of the method of measuring; the longer measurements were probably taken from dead birds lying prone, the shorter estimates from live birds. This seemed at first to be an annoying but trivial detail. However, on long-necked birds such as the American bittern, an estimate of the bird's length could vary by half depending on how an individual holds its neck when measured. The figures I have selected are intended as conservative estimates for an "alert" posture.

WINGSPAN, which is listed for the larger birds, is the distance between wing tips in flight.

VOICE includes vocalizations and other sounds char-

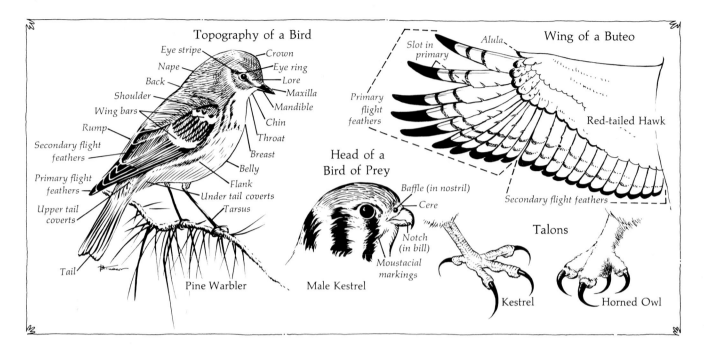

Topography of a Bird

Eye stripe
Nape
Back
Shoulder
Wing bars
Rump
Secondary flight
feathers
Primary flight
feathers
Upper tail
coverts
Tail
Crown
Eye ring
Lore
Maxilla
Mandible
Chin
Throat
Breast
Belly
Flank
Under tail coverts
Tarsus

Pine Warbler

Wing of a Buteo

Slot in
primary
Alula
Primary
flight
feathers
Red-tailed Hawk
Secondary flight feathers

**Head of a
Bird of Prey**

Baffle (in nostril)
Cere
Notch
(in bill)
Moustacial
markings

Male Kestrel

Talons

Kestrel
Horned Owl

acteristically given in winter by the species in our region. No two persons attempting to duplicate or describe a birdcall would do so identically. I have attempted onomatopoetic syllables which I hope most accurately and least ludicrously represent the sounds. **RANGE IN OUR REGION** suggests in what parts of our region the species is present. As will be obvious, the breeding and wintering ranges of many birds extend considerably beyond our region. The statement of range concentrates on the schedule of seasonal movements within the Carolinas and nearby states. **HABITAT** is a major consideration in locating and identifying birds. Most species show a preference for a special combination of terrain and vegetation that provides optimal living conditions. These associated factors give access to food and shelter and form the physiographic components of the species' ecological niche. For some, this window on life's opportunities is narrow and specialized, perhaps to the extent that slight changes to the habitat endanger their existence. Others exploit habitats that must be defined broadly.

The naturalist keys his expectations to the habitat and knows in advance which birds he might find there. A wren low to the ground in moist woods is probably a winter wren, for the house wren is absent from our region in winter, and the Carolina wren favors well-drained fencerows and clearings. We see the bobwhite running on the ground, not soaring in the sky. The *place* in which a bird is seen tells much about its life style and identity.

A natural history profile explains the principal features of each bird's winter ecology in our region and in many cases touches on the folk and historic associations of the species. The procurement of food, the relationships to other organisms in the habitat, and the important elements in life style and appearance are covered. Nesting habits are mentioned in cases where breeding activities begin in winter or are otherwise relevant to winter ecology.

Nomenclature and Taxonomy

Each species of bird, or any other form of life, has a scientific name consisting of two words: a generic name and a specific epithet. The generic term is always capitalized, and the specific epithet is not; thus, the red-bellied woodpecker is universally recognized by the scientific name *Centurus carolinus*. Common names and the barriers of language can not obscure the bird's identity when it is referred to in that manner. Folk and common names vary with time and locality and can result in confusion. The bobwhite quail, for example, is often called partridge in our region, while the same name may be applied to the ruffed grouse in New England. Technically, the term is reserved for an Old World subgroup within the family Phasianidae and is not correctly applied to any native North American species.

As well as providing an unmistakable identifier, the scientific name often suggests a significant characteristic. The white-breasted nuthatch, for example, is formally known as *Sitta carolinensis*, the specific epithet *carolinensis* suggesting that it is principally a southern bird. On the other hand, its congener, the red-breasted nuthatch, *Sitta canadensis*, prefers the more northerly latitudes its scientific name implies.

The scientific and common names used in this book are those presently adopted by the American Ornithologists' Union, the association of professional ornithologists. A committee of the AOU designates the official nomenclature and taxonomy of American birds. That committee has recently reclassified several of the birds included in this book, and changes in the official common and scientific names have resulted. The new names are used, and the former official common names are shown parenthetically. Folk names, of course, remain a matter of local preference.

Within each of the four chapters of this book the birds are arranged in generally accepted taxonomic order. The levels in the taxonomic hierarchy proceed from species to genus to family to order to class. Closely similar species are grouped in a genus of members sharing a large number of characteristics, the genera considered to share an adequate number of characteristics are grouped into a family, and groups of related families are organized into orders. The world's twenty-seven orders of birdlife unite to form the class Aves.

As an example, the cardinal, sole member of the genus *Cardinalis*, shares with other members of the family Fringillidae a stout, conical bill suitable for cracking seeds. The Fringillidae and some other families have three toes forward and one to the rear and are thus adapted to perching in trees. These families form the order Passeriformes, the perching birds. The Passeriformes may have little in common with some other orders beyond the basic Aves characteristics of egg laying, scaled skin on the feet, and modified scales, called feathers, on the rest of the body.

The taxonomic ranking is adopted by science because it reflects the degree of evolutionary advancement or crudeness of each order; the loons, order Gaviiformes, are held to be the most primitive, and the perching birds, order Passeriformes, the most advanced. Evolutionary advancement is measured inversely with the degree of specialization. A high degree of specialization indicates primitiveness, whereas the more generalized life styles bespeak advancement. Specialization narrows the opportunities of an organism's life style while generalization broadens these horizons and leads to greater adaptability. When a disturbance threatens the habitat, those forms of life that can not adapt to the change perish. For the more versatile, the same disturbance may present an opportunity rather than a threat. Certainly the birds of North America have not, in recent geologic times, faced a more fundamental disturbance than that visited upon the continent by European man. The more adaptable birds have struck their balance with human civilization, and some have even profited by the relationship. The less versatile have retreated into their dwindling wild places.

It may be more than coincidence that of the continent's twenty resident orders of birdlife, the two most advanced form the entire population of the chapter of this book entitled "At the Feeder." After being introduced by the woodpeckers, penultimate in evolutionary development, the chapter is dominated by the perching birds. I suggest that evolution has "trained" these generalists to capitalize on changes in their environment and has given them the adaptability to trust and mistrust the right humans.

Orders, Families and Subfamilies

The orders, families and subfamilies of birdlife represented in this book are listed and described below. Several families occur in more than one chapter; fringillids, for instance, are found in "At the Feeder" as well as in "Farther Afield." The families in each order are listed in unbroken taxonomic sequence regardless of their distribution among the four chapters of the book. Where an order contains a single North American family, the order and family are discussed together. Only one family, Accipitridae (the kites, hawks and eagles), is broken into subfamilies.

ORDER FALCONIFORMES

Vultures, Hawks and Falcons

The Falconiformes are birds of prey who hunt by daylight. All possess the heavy, hooked beaks, strong feet and curved talons required by their predatory life styles. The sexes typically appear similar, and females are usually larger than males. Juvenile plumages differ from those of adults, and variations in color (light and dark phases) are common. Because these birds eat "high on the food chain," many are imperiled by agricultural poisons which have accumulated in the tissues of their prey.

FAMILY CATHARTIDAE

The American Vultures

The American vultures are large soaring birds who scavenge carrion. Their heads are naked to inhibit growth of bacteria. The wings are broad, long and tipped with slotted primary feathers to facilitate soaring flight.

It is now firmly established that the vultures are valuable scavengers whose function is the hygenic removal of dead animals. Early in this century, vultures were thought to contribute to the spread of anthrax by eating the flesh of cattle that had died from the disease, then distributing the virus in their excreta. Thirty-five hundred black and turkey vultures were killed on a single Texas ranch in 1919 under this assumption. The theory was debunked with the discovery that the anthrax virus is actually destroyed in the turkey vulture's digestive tract.

Direct persecution has been greatly reduced, but populations of vultures are steadily declining. Health ordinances requiring the immediate burial of dead animals deprive the vultures of access to carrion. And much of the carrion they do find is at the shoulders of highways, imperiling the vultures because they must take off into the wind even if that happens to take them into the path of an onrushing automobile.

There are six species in the family, three of which breed in North America. The turkey vulture and the black vulture are common in our region, but the magnificent California condor, whose wings span eleven feet, hangs above the brink of extinction, with fewer than forty individuals remaining. An extinct member, *Terratornes*, who soared over western North America on twelve-foot wings, was one of the world's largest flying birds and may have been the "thunderbird" of American Indian legend.

The term "buzzard" is a misnomer. It was applied to the North American vultures because of their resemblance in flight to certain Old World soaring hawks still called by that name.

FAMILY ACCIPITRIDAE

Kites, Hawks and Eagles

This family is composed of diurnal birds of prey. It is divided into eight subfamilies of divergent form and hunting adaptation; members of three subfamilies winter with us. There are 205 accipitrid species ranging over the entire world except for the polar regions.

SUBFAMILY ACCIPITRINAE

Wood Hawks

The wood hawks are small to medium-sized diurnal raptors who feed mainly on birds. The short, rounded wings and long tails adapt the Accipitrinae to pursuing birds through trees, forests being their preferred habitat. Immatures wear plumage very different from that of adults. There are about fifty species in this widely distributed subfamily. The three occurring in North America grade in size from the mighty goshawk, an uncommon and secretive raptor of the far north who visits our region on rare occasions in winter, to the medium-sized Cooper's hawk, to the robin-sized male sharp-shinned hawk. The females are larger than the males and are only slightly smaller than the males of the next larger species.

The Accipitrinae are characterized by bold, tenacious pursuit of prey and by swift, agile flight powered by rapid bursts of wingbeats alternating with glides.

SUBFAMILY CIRCINAE

Harriers

There are seventeen species in this cosmopolitan subfamily, but only one, the marsh hawk, breeds in North America. Harriers have long, narrow wings held at a pronounced dihedral angle in flight. The tails are long and the bodies are slender. A facial disc of feathers, probably functioning as an aid to hearing, give the harriers an owllike appearance. The hunting technique is a tireless quartering of open fields and marshes from a few feet above the ground. Long legs adapt the harriers to pursuing rodents and snakes on the ground when necessary.

SUBFAMILY BUTEONINAE

Soaring Hawks and Eagles

The soaring hawks are adapted to riding the air currents for long, leisurely flights without flapping. The wings are long, broad and rounded, and the slotted primary flight feathers are spread like fingers to give extra lift in soaring flight. Widely fanned tails and robust bodies complete the flight silhouette. Mammals, mostly rodents, are the principal prey of this group. When not soaring in search of prey, the Buteoninae rest on exposed hunting perches, often near the edge of woods.

FAMILY PANDIONIDAE

Osprey

The globally-distributed osprey is the single species that constitutes the family Pandionidae. Some authorities hold that the osprey should be ranked only as a subfamily of the Accipitridae; others maintain that the presence of a reversible outer toe supports the separate family classification.

FAMILY FALCONIDAE

Caracaras and Falcons

The caracaras are long-legged, vulturelike scavengers who are actually closely related to the falcons, according to bird taxonomists, though any resemblance between the two groups in form or behavior is difficult to see. Caracaras are tropical birds of the western hemisphere with a single species, sometimes called Audubon's caracara, occurring in the United States.

The falcons are fast-flying birds of prey who hunt by taking birds on the wing, striking with explosive force often at the end of a long dive. Falcons' wings are long, swept back and pointed; the bodies are streamlined; and the tails are held narrow at the tip. The openings of the nostrils have special baffles to permit breathing at high speed. The bills are notched for grasping and breaking the necks of prey in a coup de grace. There are fifty-eight species of falcons ranging over all continents except Antarctica; nine are native to North America. Many species are critically endangered by environmental poisoning and by the stealing of eyases (nestlings) for falconry. A single species, the sparrow hawk, is numerous enough to be predictably seen inland in our region. The rare North American peregrine is regularly sighted on its coastal migration route in the Carolinas and Virginia and at Cape May, New Jersey, as well as inland along the Blue Ridge Mountains. The merlin or pigeon hawk is intermediate between the peregrine and the kestrel in size and in numbers.

ORDER GALLIFORMES

Scratching Birds

The gallinaceous, or scratching, birds are chickenlike land fowl characterized by short, stout, decurved bills and strong legs which serve as the principal means of locomotion and food procurement. The pectoral muscles are designed for short bursts of speed as in making escape flights, since emergencies are the only occasions on which most Galliformes take to the air. The poor supply of blood to the flight muscle reduces the ability to sustain flight and produces the "white meat" for which game and domestic members of the family are prized as table birds.

FAMILY MELEAGRIDIDAE

Turkeys

There are only two species of turkeys; both are native to the Americas. Like other Galliformes, turkeys are land birds who feed and live principally on the ground. Turkeys have the highly developed legs and the poor supply of blood to the pectoral muscles that are characteristic of the gallinaceous birds.

FAMILY TETRAONIDAE
Grouse

The grouse are medium-sized scratching birds with plump bodies and short, rounded wings which produce a startling WHIRRRRR when bursting into flight. The feet and nostrils are covered with feathers; in some species the stiff bristles along the toes elongate in winter to form snowshoes. The tails are short.

FAMILY PHASIANIDAE
Quail, Partridges and Pheasants

The Phasianidae are small to large scratching birds with tails ranging from short to long and ornate. The males of some species sport colorful, lustrous, often iridescent plumage. The Indian pea fowl and the ringnecked pheasant are two familiar alien members of the family. The ringneck is established in our region mainly in coastal enclaves. The bobwhite quail is the principal representative in the uplands of the region.

ORDER CICONIIFORMES
Herons and Their Allies

This order is composed of long-legged wading birds with long necks and long bills specialized for particular types of aquatic feeding. Included are the ibises, wood ibises, spoonbills and flamingoes, as well as the herons, bitterns and egrets. The cranes are *not* included. There are four North American families, of which only the Ardeidae are represented in our region in winter.

FAMILY ARDEIDAE
Herons, Egrets and Bitterns

In flight the members of this family carry their necks retracted in an S-curve with the heads resting just above the chests. This characteristic easily distinguishes the Ardeidae from the cranes, family Gruidae, who carry their necks extended in flight. Wading in the shallows of coastal marshes and inland ponds the world over, the Ardeidae thrust with their long, flexible necks and daggerlike beaks at fish, crustaceans, snakes and frogs. The length of the legs of a species suggests the depth of the water in which it is adapted to fishing.

Egrets differ from herons in that during the mating season egrets develop ornate plumes known as aigrettes. This finery was in high demand by the millinery trade near the turn of the century, and the snowy and common egrets were shot nearly to extinction. Bitterns are effectively camouflaged with vertical patterns which enable them to simulate reedy marsh plants.

The Ardeidae are colonial nesters, and in winter they occupy communal roosts. Their voices are unmusical croaks and squawks. There are sixty-four species worldwide, thirteen in North America, and three that winter in the uplands of our region.

ORDER CHARADRIIFORMES
Shorebirds, Gulls and Alcids

This order embraces the shorebirds as well as the gulls, terns, skimmers, jaegers and skuas and the alcids (auks, murres and puffins). All but a few species are aquatic, and most are associated with the seas and shores rather than with fresh water. The members are diverse in form, being fitted by evolution to exploit the great variety of feeding opportunities afforded by the waters of the world. The wings of most are long, the colors are muted, and the sexes appear similar.

FAMILY CHARADRIIDAE
Plovers, Turnstones and Surfbirds

The Charadriidae are grouped with five other families into a major subdivision of the order Charadriiformes known as the shorebirds. Other families of shorebirds include the jacanas, the oystercatchers, the sandpipers, the avocets and the phalaropes. Charadriidae have small to medium-sized, plump bodies and short bills enlarged near the tips. The necks are short, as are the horizontally held tails. The hind toe is lacking or vestigial. Running swiftly on medium to long legs, the Charadriidae feed on marine invertebrates on the beaches, and on worms and insects in the uplands. A distraction display, in which the adult feigns injury to lure intruders from the nest, is a behavioral practice of many species in this family.

Sixty-three species comprise this cosmopolitan family. Sixteen breed in the United States, of which one species, the killdeer, occupies the uplands of our region.

FAMILY SCOLOPACIDAE

Woodcocks, Curlews and Sandpipers

The family Scolopacidae is a large and cosmopolitan group of eighty-two species, thirty-three of which are found in North America. Most of the Scolopacidae occupy habitats on beaches or in coastal marshes. We are concerned with two species, the common snipe and the American woodcock, which have left the coastal habitats in favor of the uplands. The two share many similarities in form and in the pattern of their markings, but they differ in their principal ecological adaptations. The snipe is a diurnal feeder of the open wetlands; the woodcock is a nocturnal bird of the moist woodlands. Both probe into the wet soils with their long bills for invertebrates. In the United States they are the only members of the family that are hunted legally.

The Scolopacidae typically have long legs and long bills for probing in mud or sand, and they are strong fliers. Many perform notable display flights, none of which are more spectacular than the courtship aerobatics of the snipe and the woodcock.

ORDER COLUMBIFORMES

FAMILY COLUMBIDAE

Pigeons and Doves

The order Columbiformes includes the doves and pigeons (the terms being synonymous), and the extinct, flightless dodos of the Mascarene Islands. The pigeons and doves, 290 species strong, comprise the family Columbidae and are distributed throughout the temperate world. The Columbidae are small to medium-sized land birds. The bluebird-sized ground dove of the southern United States and South America is the smallest, and the Victoria crowned pigeon of New Guinea is largest, measuring thirty-three inches.

The Columbidae wear the same plumage in all seasons, and the sexes are similar, the females of some species being slightly duller. Iridescence and scaled patterns, especially around the neck, highlight the muted plumages. A few species are crested. The wings are pointed, and all members are strong, swift fliers, though only a few migrate. Columbidae drink with the bill immersed and the head down, a trait shared with only one other family, the Old World sand grouse. Newly hatched young are fed "pigeon's milk," a curdy secretion of the lining of the adults' crop. All species nod their heads when walking.

There are seventeen species of pigeons and doves in the United States, three of which are introduced. Several species were shot nearly to extinction in the nineteenth century, and the once-numerous passenger pigeon succumbed to the mindless persecution. The mourning dove, a native, and the introduced rock dove, or street pigeon, are both numerous in our region. The ground dove is occasionally seen in our region but resides principally in Florida and along the Gulf Coast.

ORDER STRIGIFORMES

Owls

Owls are mostly nocturnal predators with large heads, short necks and strong talons with two toes facing forward, two rearward. The very large eyes do not move within their sockets but are fixed aiming forward. Three-dimensional vision is achieved by moving the head back and forth laterally to gain "motion parallax," an effect which shows the distance to an object by its apparent motion relative to closer and more distant objects. The flight feathers have soft edges to muffle the sounds of flight. Nocturnal owls rely heavily on hearing to locate prey, and many can do so in total darkness, when the extraordinary light-gathering power of their eyes is of no use. Facial discs of sensory feathers sharpen the hearing of nocturnal owls in some manner not fully understood. Diurnal owls, such as those living in the far north where there is continuous daylight during summer, need to rely more on sight than on hearing and consequently lack facial discs. All owls regurgitate the undigestible parts of their prey in compact pellets of characteristic shape and size which, if found, yield information on the diet.

There are two families within the order Strigiformes: the barn owls, family Tytonidae, and the "typical" owls, family Strigidae. Of the world's eleven tytonids, a single species, the common barn owl, resides in North America. It is a totally nocturnal raptor with perhaps the world's most acute sense of hearing. Because it is nearly voiceless, or at least because it rarely uses its voice, the bird is seldom heard. It is seen only if found nesting, usually in an abandoned building. Since it is so difficult to locate by sight or sound, its status in much of the United States is uncertain. The barn owl no doubt resides in our region, and any record of the bird should be shared with other naturalists. The whitish appearance combined with a heart-shaped facial disc are diagnostic.

FAMILY STRIGIDAE

Typical Owls

The family Strigidae contains 123 species of typical owls, 17 occurring in North America. Some have ear tufts, or "horns," which serve no auditory function but do provide camouflage. Most species are nocturnal; some are diurnal. Many members of this family are strongly vocal, issuing characteristic hoots and wails which provide the principal method of owl identification. The prey is almost entirely small mammals, usually rodents, though some birds are taken.

ORDER CORACIIFORMES

FAMILY ALCEDINIDAE

Kingfishers

The kingfishers are small to medium-sized land birds adapted to catching fish. Their heads and beaks appear to be oversized in proportion to their bodies, and it is easy to see that they are related to the hornbills. Being "top-heavy," the kingfishers are fitted for diving head-first into the water to catch fish swimming near the surface. The massive head and stout neck take the impact. The bird's feet and legs are small and weak, and the outer toes are fused together in some species.

There are eighty-seven species of kingfishers enjoying cosmopolitan distribution. Only two nest north of the Rio Grande; they are the belted and the green kingfishers. The belted is the sole representative in the United States outside of Texas, but it ranges extensively over most of temperate North America.

Kingfishers are strong fliers, though most flights cover short distances. They are solitary birds seen singly except during the nesting season.

ORDER PICIFORMES
FAMILY PICIDAE
Woodpeckers

Of the twenty-two woodpeckers in North America north of Mexico, seven live in the Carolinas and nearby states. All members of the family are equipped with a heavy, wood-chiseling bill anchored to thick cranial bones. The tongue is fixed by a bony hinge at the base of the bill and extends rearward between the skull and the scalp, over the top of the head and back into the mouth. The tongue can typically extend over twice the head's length to help perform the specialized function of each species of woodpecker. Several species have tongues tipped with rearward-pointing barbs for fishing grubs out of their galaries in the deadwood. The flicker's is coated with a sticky mucous for capturing ants, and the sapsucker's has a brush for lapping fluid out of the wells drilled into bark.

The flight of woodpeckers is swift and direct. Rapid wingbeats alternate with moments when the birds hurtle through the air, bulletlike, with the wings folded at their sides. The result is an undulating flight path, usually ending in an upward swoop. Most woodpeckers alight against vertical surfaces, gripping the bark on a tree trunk with two toes forward and two to the rear, and propping themselves with their tail feathers. The flicker often perches across branches like the passerine birds.

Woodpeckers nest and roost in cavities excavated into deadwood. The exception is the red-cockaded, the only bird in the world known to drill habitually into living wood.

Some woodpeckers have developed highly specialized life styles. Extreme specialization leads to vulnerability, inability to adjust to environmental change. As a result, one woodpecker, the ivorybill, would have been included in this section had the book been written a hundred years earlier, but it is now extinct (at least as a breeding species in our region). It lived on the larvae of a certain beetle in the wetland hardwoods. When its habitat was destroyed by logging and draining, the ivorybill, the largest woodpecker in the world, could not find an alternate diet or habitat. Similarly, the red-cockaded woodpecker was decimated by the cutting of the vast longleaf pine forests that once covered over a million acres of a region extending from New Jersey to Georgia. The bird is now on the official Rare and Endangered Species List, with perhaps only three thousand individuals remaining.

The vocalizations of woodpeckers are varied but typically loud and repetitive. The birds also "rap" with one another by drumming on hardened wood, communicating with a code characteristic to each species.

ORDER PASSERIFORMES
Perching Birds

This is the largest and most evolutionarily advanced order of birdlife. Its members have feet well adapted for perching; three toes face forward and an elongated one extends to the rear. Passerine birds have adapted their form and habits to a wide variety of life styles and feeding opportunities, and as a consequence, the order is subdivided into fifty-seven families worldwide. Twenty-five families breed in North America, and eighteen have representatives wintering in our region.

FAMILY TYRANNIDAE
Tyrant Flycatchers

The tyrant flycatchers are small, insectivorous birds, who typically capture their prey in short flying sorties from exposed hunting perches. The bills are rather broad and slightly hooked at the tip. Stiff whiskerlike feathers called rictal bristles help guide the prey into the mouth. The sexes of all species of tyrannids found in the United States are garbed alike in somber grays and browns, with the single exception of the vermilion flycatcher of the extreme southwest. With the exception of the kiskadee of the lower Rio Grande Valley, all are migratory. The tails are squared at the tip, except on species with long, ornate tails, such as the scissor-tailed flycatcher.

There are in the family Tyrannidae 265 species plucking insects from the air from Alaska to Tierra del Fuego. Thirty-two species occur north of Mexico. To the consternation of even veteran birders, the family has many look-alikes whose identities can sometimes be established only by nuances of voice and behavior. The nine species in the genus *Empidonax* present the extreme of this problem.

The eastern phoebe is the only tyrannid wintering in the Carolinas and nearby states. Identifying this bird and confirming its function in the natural systems of our region is an important challenge for the naturalist.

FAMILY ALAUDIDAE
Larks

The plumage of the larks is typically a brownish camouflage to match the grasses in which they feed. The birds are small and terrestrial. The length and shape of the tails, wings and legs are too variable to characterize. The claw of the hind toe is elongated. Some species have crests or small plumes on the head.

Larks walk rather than hop and, if flushed, return to the ground, seldom to bushes or trees.

There are seventy-six species in the family, distributed primarily over Eurasia and northern Africa. The horned lark is the only member native to North America.

Larks are noted for their rich, elaborate songs. The courtship vocalizations of the Old World skylark, now introduced on Vancouver Island, have inspired some of Europe's great poets. Larks sing in flight, often from hundreds of feet in the air.

FAMILY CORVIDAE
Crows, Jays and Magpies

The corvids are medium to large birds with heavy, all-purpose bills. The wings are rounded, extending at rest only to the base of the jay's tail, nearer the tip of the crow's and raven's. The birds are gregarious and omnivorous. Predation plays a role in the feeding habits of all corvids. The vocalizations are more often raucous than musical, though some notes of the blue jay and many of the common raven are hauntingly beautiful.

There are one hundred species of corvids worldwide, fifteen in North America north of Mexico. Four species are found in our region, and all of them are year-round residents. By their calls, their craftiness, and their dominance over most other birds, the corvids always enter our perceptions of wildlife.

FAMILY PARIDAE
Titmice and Chickadees

The Paridae are a large and cosmopolitan family of more than sixty species in Europe, Asia, Africa and North America. Our region hosts only the titmice and chickadees. Other North American Paridae include the verdins and the bushtits.

Members of the Paridae family are typically fearless and friendly by nature. At least they tolerate the presence of humans and make every effort to capitalize upon it. They are also quite bold with other birds; this characteristic permits them to compete for food by quickly snatching morsels from feeding situations dominated by other birds. Most of the birds in this family nest in cavities. They typically occupy abandoned woodpecker holes and sometimes the excavations of nuthatches. Occasionally they enlarge the cavities of other birds or perhaps excavate their own.

The chickadees, smallest in the family, all have dark caps and bibs. They are bold, scolding midgets who gain with tenacity and fearlessness what their size would otherwise deny them. Only in the mountains of the Northwest do more than two species of chickadees occupy the same range. Our region is partitioned between the territories of the black-capped and Carolina chickadees approximately at the Virginia-Carolina border, with some overlap and intergrading.

The titmice are small, crested birds slightly larger than the chickadees and equally bold and vocal. Like the chickadees, they have a short, stout bill used for picking, hammering and prying. Some species can excavate into wood.

The sexes of chickadees and titmice are indistinguishable. Young chickadees resemble the adults soon after fledging; juvenile titmice are distinguished by their duller plumage.

FAMILY SITTIDAE

Nuthatches

The nuthatches are constantly on the move in search of nutmeats and insects in the forest. This family of small, stub-tailed arboreal birds is represented worldwide except in the Americas south of Mexico. Of the thirty species, four occur in North America, three of which are found in the Carolinas and nearby states. The pygmy nuthatch keeps to the mountains of the west. The white-breasted and brown-headed nest and winter in the vicinity of the Carolinas, and the red-breasted winters in our region.

The wings of nuthatches, when at rest, typically extend to the tips of the tails; they are long and pointed in flight. The flight profile undulates like that of the woodpeckers and is strong and direct. The tails are short and squared and usually show some white. The bills are long and pointed. The heads seem slightly oversized in comparison with the compact bodies.

The nuthatch's practice of moving headfirst down a tree trunk is unique. I have seen the white-breasted run headlong down a tree to catch a falling morsel of suet. The bird, apparently unconcerned with gravity or with the concept of up versus down, moves without using the tail as a prop. No other arboreal bird maneuvers against vertical surfaces of trees without propping with the tail. Nuthatches place one foot before the other and hitch along the bark, balancing against the strong rearward toes. The feet are large and powerful, but not always visible, because the legs are kept drawn against the body.

Nuthatches respond readily to offerings of suet and sunflower seed. They carry off more than they can use, and store the excess in a cache for leaner times. Other birds and squirrels often get the benefit of the nuthatches' savings accounts. Natural food is principally bark-dwelling insects during the warmer months, shifting to acorns, nuts and pine seeds in winter. The name originated in England centuries ago when "to hatch" meant "to hack open." The birds were seen wedging nuts into crevices in bark and opening them with powerful blows of their sharp bills. These same bills can excavate a nesting cavity into a hard cedar fence post, which I've watched the brown-headed do. I've also witnessed the white-breasted punch in a knothole on a living white oak and round out a homesite.

FAMILY CERTHIIDAE

Creepers

The creepers are small, slender arboreal birds with stiff tail feathers which they use as a prop while foraging for insects and arachnids in crevices in the bark of tree trunks. The feet have long claws and great endurance for climbing and clinging. The bills are long and, in many species, decurved. Plumage typically matches the bark of trees. The voices are variable and not strong. Most creepers are solitary, and few are migratory.

There are seventeen species distributed worldwide except for South America and the polar regions. A single species, the brown creeper, represents the family in North America.

FAMILY TROGLODYTIDAE

Wrens

The wrens are brownish birds, small but voluble, with tails held erect. Coloration is usually fine dark stripings against a brown or buff background. The bills are long and slender, often curved downward. With one exception, an Old World species, the wrens are birds of the Americas. Sixty-three species penetrate a variety of life niches from Patagonia to Alaska. Many thrive in tropical vegetation. Ten species breed in the United States and Canada. We are concerned with only two species in the Carolinas and nearby states in winter.

The family name comes from a Greek word meaning "cave dweller" because wrens nest in cavities. The accommodations may be fashioned by nature or by man. Abandoned woodpecker holes, rock crevices (in arid regions) or tussocks of grass may provide homes for some wrens. Others make use of a variety of man-made shelters not limited to birdhouses.

Wrens have insinuated themselves deeply into the human psyche and folklore. The Old World wren was fabled to have gained an avian kingship by flying to the greatest height in a competition held to determine which species would rule. The wren prevailed by the simple expedient of riding an eagle's back as high as the great bird could soar, then sprinting for the title. The Cherokee Indians suspected wrens of being spies slipping about and nosing into everyone's business. Many of us have experiences with the inquisitive Carolina wren that could easily sustain this suspicion.

In song the wrens excel. Probably no other birds produce such volume from so little body. Wrens don't just begin to sing; they burst into song. Writing in 1885 of the winter wren's territorial song, the great naturalist John Burroughs said that the cadence "seems to go off like a musical alarm." And somewhere in the mind of anyone who savors his walks along the woods' edge is the experience of being startled by a burst of the Carolina wren's gaiety.

FAMILY MIMIDAE

Catbirds, Thrashers and Mockingbirds

The Mimidae are songbirds of moderate size and modest coloring, the sexes being typically indistinguishable. The tails are long, approximately the length of the body; the wings are short and rounded. The bills are long, slender and, in many species, curved slightly downward.

Any deficiencies in plumage color in this family are more than balanced by excellence of voice. Many Mimidae sing almost continuously, some not missing a note when they take flight. Their ability to reproduce sounds they hear has earned them the common appellation "mimic thrushes." A prominent theory as to why these birds engage in vocal mimicry is that, being continuous singers, they need the borrowed material. They are capable of extensive composition but often augment their repertoire with the songs of other birds and with nonavian sounds they hear.

The eastern Mimidae exploit several habitats. The catbird inhabits the deciduous understory; the brown thrasher, the briar thickets and hedgerows; the mockingbird, our lawns and woods' edges. All feed and breed near the ground, the mocker occasionally rising to sing from the top of a cedar or a TV antenna. Insects, berries and other soft foods are preferred. The birds are solitary by nature, but families feed together for a few weeks after the young fledge. The wintering members of this family are almost always seen singly.

The family resides entirely in the Americas. Thirty-two species are listed, ten breeding north of Mexico. Of the three species in the Carolinas and nearby states, only the catbird migrates in winter to sea-moderated warmths of the coastal and southern extremes of our region. The brown thrasher migrates but includes our whole region in its wintering range. The mockingbird is a sedentary year-round resident.

FAMILY TURDIDAE

Robins, Thrushes and Bluebirds

The Turdidae are plump birds with short, squared tails. The wings vary from short and rounded to longer and pointed. The bills are modestly long, slender and stout. The sexes in many species are nearly indistinguishable, the bluebird being our most notable exception. Courtship is simple, usually preceded by vigorous territorial assertions by the males, who recognize the females more by their behavior than by their appearance. The plumage is usually of muted grays or browns, again excepting that of the bluebird, whose dazzling cobalt blue places it among the most colorful of North American birds. The young of all Turdidae, and in some cases the adults, have spotted breasts.

There are 306 thrushes, as the members of the family are commonly called, who are distributed over much of the globe. Most are Old World species. Twenty-three inhabit the Americas, and fourteen breed in North America. Fortunately, many of these are tolerant of man and have struck profitable bargains with human civilization. The robin and the eastern bluebird occupy prominent positions in our perceptions of wildlife and represent to us not only the Turdidae but the natural world in general.

The hermit thrush, the eastern bluebird and the robin are the only members of the family who commonly winter in the Carolinas and nearby states. Most members of the family are strongly migratory, and all but the robins and bluebirds migrate at night.

Of the Turdidae who winter in our region, only the robin is a noted vocalist, though even it is largely mute on the wintering grounds. The bluebird's slurred whistles echo gently against the winter woods, coming more as occasional whispers than as bursts of song. I've never heard a hermit thrush utter a note here in winter. It is said, though, that his song electrifies the north woods during the breeding season. In spring when the other members of the family head north, passing through our region or nesting here, their songs fill our heads. The robin welcomes the soft summer nights with ringing choruses at dusk. And the wood thrush gives us the purest, clearest notes of any living creature.

FAMILY SYLVIIDAE
Kinglets and Gnatcatchers

"Song gave the sylviids the name of warbler in the old world—and they merit it far more than our thin-voiced American wood warblers, an entirely different family for whom the name was borrowed," writes Austin Rand, an authority on this family. We don't hear much sylviid song in our region because, of the three species occurring in eastern North America, only the blue-gray gnatcatcher nests with us, and it is the least vocal. The two kinglets nest to the north of our region and fill the northern spruce forests across the continent with the rollicking territorial songs of which Rand speaks.

The kinglets winter throughout the Carolinas and nearby states. The song is absent on the wintering grounds, but the ruby-crowned's scolding chatter attends our every walk through the second-growth woods. The golden-crowned's faint, high-pitched lisps are caught only by the trained listener.

All North American sylviids are tiny—hardly a half size larger than the ruby-throated hummingbird. The bills are short and thin. The colors are the drab grays and olive-browns of their winter habitats. The kinglets have stubby tails; the gnatcatchers have long, thin tails held gracefully erect. All are nervous little birds constantly in motion as they scan the winter twigs and bark for insects. The kinglets flit several times a second from twig to trunk, seizing flying insects in short, erratic flights. They hover briefly and assume every possible contorted position as they move through the trees in a ceaseless search for food. Both kinglets have the distinctive habit of flicking their wings in such a way that it is difficult to tell if they have jumped or flown from one twig to the next.

The ruby-crowned kinglet often responds to an offering of beef suet or a mixture of cornmeal, bacon fat and peanut butter and is therefore included in "At the Feeder." I am not aware of an instance of the golden-crowned's acceptance of a human's offering. It prefers to pick its nits from high in the pines. Both birds are gregarious, and the feeding flocks often mix. Other wintering birds such as pine warblers, red-breasted nuthatches and brown creepers sometimes join the kinglets in feeding forays that must devastate the sparse populations of wintering insects.

FAMILY MOTACILLIDAE
Pipits and Wagtails

Of the forty-eight species in this principally Old World family, three breed in North America. They are the yellow wagtail, a bird of the extreme North, and the Sprague's and water pipits. The water pipit winters across the southern United States, and the Sprague's winters in Texas and Louisiana. All species have long, dark tails with white outer tail feathers. The bodies are slender and sparrow-sized; the bills are warblerlike, thin spikes. Motacillidae walk on the ground without hopping and fly in compact flocks.

FAMILY BOMBYCILLIDAE
Waxwings

Two of this family's three members reside in North America; the third is Asian. The species are basically similar in form, demeanor and ecology. Their soft-textured plumage is muted but brightly trimmed. All have erectile crests, yellow terminal tail bands, and red, waxy tips to the secondary flight feathers. The cedar waxwing winters in or near the Carolinas; the Bohemian is a more northern bird.

FAMILY LANIIDAE
Shrikes

The shrikes are small predaceous birds with hooked beaks. Unlike the hawks and owls, shrikes do not have highly developed talons for holding and tearing prey. To compensate, they impale their victims on thorns as an aid in butchering. The seventy-four species in the family are distributed worldwide. Only two, the northern and the loggerhead, reside in North America. The loggerhead is the sole representative of the family in our region.

FAMILY STURNIDAE
Starlings

Starlings are small to medium-sized birds with heavy, pointed bills and short tails. Stout feet and legs adapt them to foraging as well in the trees as on the ground, where they walk rather than hop. The plumage is typically dark and glossy, often spotted. Wattles decorate the heads of some species. Most are noisy; some, such as the mynas, are excellent mimics. Communal nesting and roosting are practiced by many members of the family.

The term "starling" is applied to all Sturnidae. The family originated in the Old World, and the native ranges of its 112 species are in Europe, Asia, Africa and Australia. Three species, the common starling and two mynas, have been introduced into North America. The common starling has proliferated on this and other continents to the detriment of man and the native birdlife.

FAMILY PARULIDAE
Wood Warblers

The wood warblers are small birds with slender, straight, pointed bills. In their spring plumage, the brightly colored males shimmer like gems in the crowns of the trees. On their northward migration in early spring, the wood warblers practice their distinctive territorial calls and can be located in the new foliage by sound more easily than by sight. The fall plumages of some are vastly different from the nuptial garb. The plumage of the females usually bears some resemblance to that of the males and is duller.

The members of the family are almost entirely insectivorous, a fact which accounts in part for their long seasonal migrations. A trek twice yearly between breeding grounds in the Yukon and a South American rain forest is not uncommon.

The name "wood warbler" is used to differentiate the strictly American family Parulidae from the Old World warblers in the family Sylviidae. The Parulidae are a very large family. Some thirty-seven species can be observed in our region during the year, and fourteen predictably nest in or near the Carolinas.

Wood warblers are most vocal and visible in springtime. An authority I have long relied on to help interpret my observations on the family describes them as "gaily garbed warm weather birds." Only the four most intrepid species winter in our region. They serve during the severest months to keep us in contact with this family of tremendously important controllers of woodland insects. We know that the same individuals who wolf tiny mouthfuls of cornmeal, bacon fat and peanut butter from our windowsill feeder will don their brilliant colors in late winter to become one of spring's first signals. Soon their kinsmen will join them from the south, and the full rush of spring will be on.

FAMILY PLOCEIDAE
Weaver Finches

The weaver finches comprise a very large Old World family of 263 species ranging throughout Eurasia, Africa, Australia and islands in the Pacific Ocean. The Ploceidae resemble native North American finches but have shorter legs and stouter conical bills. In most species the wings are short and square-tipped. Many members of the family are colonial nesters. Ploceid architecture includes exquisitely woven flask-shaped hanging nests, spherical structures and multi-unit apartments. The nests of the two species that have become established in North America are inartistic heaps of debris. The English or house sparrow is the sole representative in our region.

FAMILY ICTERIDAE

Meadowlarks, Blackbirds and Orioles

Icterids are a family of medium-sized birds diverse in song, plumage and feeding adaptations. The upper ridge of the icterid's characteristically straight and pointed bill separates the feathers on the forehead and appears to be level with the top of the bird's head. The members of this family have long bills, except the cowbird and bobolink, whose stout, conical, fringillidlike bills are adapted for cracking seeds. The males are colorful, but the hues are limited to iridescent blacks with yellows and oranges.

Although the orioles, meadowlarks and grackles have the head and bill shape characteristic of icterids, they use their feeding implements in a variety of ways. The meadowlark and the orchard oriole have extra strength in the muscles that open their bills. The meadowlark jabs into the sod, pries open a hole, and extracts a worm. The orchard oriole opens wells in fruit to get the juices and often the pulp. Grackles open acorns with a ridge on the inside of the upper bill. The red-winged blackbird can slit reeds with its pointed bill to expose grubs.

In song also the icterids show variability. On its breeding grounds, the bobolink's notes tinkle like glass wind chimes. The unmusical squawks and squeaks of grackles and rusty blackbirds wintering in large flocks in our region contrast with the springtime songs of orioles and meadowlarks.

Territorial and nuptial displays are readily observable in our region. Toward spring, when the common grackles begin to pair, the male displays his iridescent purple neck feathers, points his bill to the sky, and in ecstasy covers his eyes with the nictitating membrane and delivers a metallic squeak. The redwing hunches his shoulders to display his gaudy epaulettes and puts his whole being into a slightly more musical screech. Sunrise on a spring morning catches the golden breast of the meadowlark as he sings brilliant notes from his fence post. Best dressed and most musical of all icterids, the orioles provide striking springtime song and color.

The nearly one hundred species of icterids live only in the Americas. Nineteen live north of Mexico. Some, like the bobolink, undertake intercontinental migrations; others find no need for separate wintering and nesting habitats.

FAMILY FRINGILLIDAE

Cardinals, Finches, Towhees, Grosbeaks, Sparrows

The fringillids are the largest family of North American birds. There are 79 species north of Mexico, and 426 worldwide on all continents except Antarctica and Australia. The heavy, conical, seed-cracking bill is the family's unifying characteristic. Beyond that, the fringillids are diverse in form and life style and occupy a variety of habitats. Many feed on or near the ground; others glean the tops of forest canopies. Swamps, prairies, seacoasts and highlands have all been exploited by the fringillids.

The family can be divided into two groups, the colorful and the plain. Some of the continent's most richly hued birds comprise the first group: notably the cardinal, the grosbeaks and the buntings and, less spectacularly, the finches, crossbills and towhees. Where the colors are bright on the male, they tend to be subdued on the female. In contrast, the second group, principally the sparrows, is characterized by muted, protective coloration. The sexes are usually similar in the sparrow group.

The design of their bills adapts the fringillids to a diet of seeds. Many eat insects in the warmer months and turn to cracking seeds when cold eliminates the insects. The mandible closes against the maxilla along a "mouth" line angling sharply downward at the base. This buttressed structure adds power as well as an extra cutting edge to the bill. The evening grosbeak is allegedly capable of cracking a cherry pit. The smaller finches and sparrows concentrate on the more accessible seeds of herbaceous grasses and legumes. The seeds of asters are useful to many medium-sized fringillids. The crossbills, who visit our region only occasionally, have developed specialized "pruning shear" mandibles for prying the seeds from the cones of conifers.

Chapter I

At the Feeder

grosbeak and finches

Woodpeckers *(Order Piciformes)*

FAMILY PICIDAE

COMMON FLICKER, YELLOW-SHAFTED RACE
(Formerly Yellow-Shafted Flicker)
Colaptes auratus auratus

FIELD MARKS: Generally brown with rows of black markings across the back and down the sides. Brilliant yellows flash beneath the wings in flight. A white "snowball" marking the rump is especially visible as the bird flies away from the observer. Head markings include a gray crown split laterally by a red crescent. A black bib crosses the throat. The male sports a black "moustache," as do fledglings of both sexes.
LENGTH: 10½ inches.
VOICE: A loud WICK-a-WICK-a-WICK and a ringing KEEO. Also assorted mumbled chirrings.
RANGE IN OUR REGION: Nests and winters throughout.
HABITAT: Hardwoods and open lands. Often seen on the ground.

The stomach of one common flicker yielded over five thousand ants. That testifies directly to the flicker's terrestrial feeding habits. Flickers are seen on the ground more than any other woodpecker, and their specialty is lapping ants out of fallen deadwood with a sticky tongue which can extend two inches past the tip of the bill. One species of flicker lives on the Argentine pampas, where there are no trees. The terrestrial adaptation has given the flickers longer-than-average legs for a woodpecker and has shifted them forward on the body for better balance while on the ground. As often as not, the flicker perches across a limb like a perching bird (order Passeriformes) but is still adept at clinging woodpecker-style to the side of a tree, using the tail feathers as a prop.

Autumn drives the common flicker from the northern reaches of its range. Large flocks are sometimes seen moving through the Carolinas, though the bird is common here in all seasons. Cold weather brings no apparent reduction in numbers in the southeast, though migratory movements can be significant. A flicker banded in Iowa was recovered in Louisiana.

Much of the flicker's time is given over to posturing and pronouncements. The courtship is lively and spectacular. Endless nuptial chases are accompanied by elaborate vocalizations. Several flickers may join together in a dance, weaving the head and shoulders from side to side in accompaniment to a WICK-a-WICK-a-WICK song. I once saw five flickers noisily lacing in single file through a longleaf pine woods and perching occasionally on the trunk of a tree bearing the enlarged opening of a red-cockaded woodpecker, there to enact their ritual of dance and chant. There were three males and two females celebrating.

After courtship both sexes join in mining a cavity for a nest. Haystacks and road banks have been used. Hardwood trees are usually selected when available. From inside the hole, the birds often make an annoyed whirring sound as if excavation were not proceeding rapidly enough to satisfy the nesting urge. Once the cavity is dug, the flickers must often endure the co-ordinated assaults of pairs of starlings, who are frequently successful in evicting the legitimate occupants.

The starling is not the only peril the flicker faces. Loggerhead shrikes sometimes pirate larger insects from the flicker. The flicker was a favored prey of the peregrine falcon, now nearly extinct, who would strike from great heights at blinding speed to take advantage of this woodpecker's fondness for open spaces. Unfortunately, there is little chance that the spectacle will ever be seen again in the eastern United States.

RED-BELLIED WOODPECKER
Centurus carolinus

FIELD MARKS: Thin black and white stripes alternate across the back. White wing patches show in flight. The underparts are a dull white *occasionally* showing a faint rusty tinge. The back of the female's neck and head is red. The same marking on the male extends upward across the top of the head to the base of the bill.
LENGTH: 8½ inches.
VOICE: A loud CHAK; an ascending urgent YINK, YINK, YINK, YINK; a guttural WUCKA, WUCKA, WUCKA.
RANGE IN OUR REGION: Nests and winters throughout.
HABITAT: Woodlands of all types, from the cabbage palms of the barrier islands to the spruces of Mt. Mitchell.

"Showy," "noisy," "common," "conspicuous" are terms frequently applied to the red-bellied, our best-known medium-sized woodpecker. Common names more descriptive than red-bellied include "wood guinea" and "zebra woodpecker." The Latin name *Centurus carolinus* suggests the bird's association with the southeastern United States, although its range extends to the Mississippi and to the Great Lakes. Because it is numerous, loud and obvious, the red-bellied is often said not to be shy. However, while attempting close-up photography, I have found it excruciatingly skittish, backing hesitantly down a tree trunk toward suet, protesting loudly and tolerating *no* movement on the part of the photographer.

The flight is very strong, direct and deeply undulatting. Excess airspeed is usually bled off with a steep upward swoop, at the top of which the bird alights on the trunk of a tree, never perching on a branch. The species is weakly migratory, its seasonal movements better described as wanderings.

The red-bellied is more vegetarian than most woodpeckers. Its diet is animal and vegetable matter in roughly equal quantities. It sometimes feeds on the ground, probing the forest litter for ants and grubs, but the bird is more at home hammering dead snags for wood-boring insects. In winter the wood guinea enjoys the berries of holly, dogwood, Virginia creeper, honeysuckle and other persistent fruits. It warily but frequently accepts suet and sunflower seeds. In Florida the red-bellied often shows an unwelcome interest in ripening oranges. Hedging against hard times, it stores acorns and nuts for future use. It has been known to wedge large collections of insects into crevices in bark when more insects were available than could be eaten at a sitting.

The red-bellied shows red much more conspicuously on the head than on the belly. In fact, the name can be misleading, for the belly, under normal conditions of lighting and plumage, appears a dull white. I have one slightly underexposed photograph in which a faint reddish blush is visible, but under direct observation in bright sunlight the red on the underparts is not a reliable field mark. It is a common error to see the blazing red stripe that covers the back of the head and declare the bird a red-headed woodpecker. One comparative look at the two birds will clarify the point.

5 / At the Feeder

HAIRY WOODPECKER
Dendrocopos villosus

FIELD MARKS: The underparts are white, and a broad white stripe runs down the back. The wings have black and white stripes. The outer tail feathers are pure white. The hairy looks like the downy on a 1½ scale, but the bill is longer in proportion to the head. A red patch on the back of the male's head differentiates the sexes.
LENGTH: 7½ inches.
VOICE: A loud sharp PEEK, a trembling PEEEEEEEEK.
RANGE IN OUR REGION: Nests and winters throughout.
HABITAT: Most woodlands off the beaten track. Avoids humanity.

The hairy and the downy are strikingly similar and easily confused. The difference in size is not so great as to be always immediately obvious. The hairy is seen less often than the downy, is shier, and keeps more to the forest, though it will respond to an offering of beef suet tacked to a lawn tree.

The flight is strong and fast with deep undulations. George H. Lowery, Jr., an authority on woodpeckers, writes of the hairy, "His swift passage through the tangled foliage is a miracle of split second timing."

After a brief autumn courtship of joyful aerobatics through the forest, the sexes maintain separate wintering territories. Therefore the hairy is usually seen singly in winter, but mated pairs can be heard drumming to one another to maintain year-round contact.

Food consists of fruits (wild grape, dogwood, black gum) and insect larvae which the bird skewers on its long barbed tongue from beneath the bark. Like all woodpeckers, the hairy is a tireless protector of trees from the attacks of wood-boring insects.

Between the lid and the eye, birds have a translucent nictitating membrane which provides protection for the eye while permitting some vision. The female hairy woodpecker in the photograph has closed her nictitating membrane as her head goes forward to strike at the bark.

The hairy can be found in open pine woods, deciduous woods and hardwood swamps. It roosts and nests in cavities twenty to fifty feet up wherever timber grows in North America. It does not migrate. In most areas it is not nearly so common as the downy. Because of its shyness and its association with the deeper woods, the hairy conveys a sense of wildness. Finding and identifying the bird is a reward reserved for the careful observer. The explosively loud call is often a clue to its presence.

DOWNY WOODPECKER
Dendrocopos pubescens

FIELD MARKS: Our smallest woodpecker. White bands alternate with black in the wings at rest. There is a broad white stripe down the back. White outer tail feathers show black markings. The male has a bright red patch at the back of the head. The downy is distinguished from the larger hairy by its proportionately shorter bill and black markings on the outer tail feathers.
LENGTH: 5¾ inches.
VOICE: PEEK, PEEEEEEEK, similar to hairy's but not as loud.
RANGE IN OUR REGION: Winters and nests throughout.
HABITAT: Anywhere trees grow.

This is our smallest and most common woodpecker. Throughout its North American range, it is also the most intimate with man. Working upward on the tree trunks like a creeper, the downy grooms our pine and hardwood forests and the trees in our lawns, showing little concern for the presence of humans. Indeed, this elfin woodpecker seems to enjoy a game of peek-a-boo, peering at us from behind successive trees along a woodland walk. The call is a high-pitched descending giggle, sometimes a single explosive bleat.

The downy does not migrate. It combs our woodlands in all seasons, hacking into dead and diseased wood in search of wood-boring insects and their larvae. Nuts and acorns are part of its winter diet. And like all woodpeckers, the downy will accept an offering of beef suet tied to a tree. It utilizes the stored energy in the fat to help propel it through the winter forest.

In spring and autumn courtship, the male follows the female in nuptial flight, their wings fluttering through a shallow arc held at a high dihedral angle suggesting the flight of a bat. The normal flight pattern is the strong direct series of arcs characteristic of the woodpecker family. Quick whiffling wingbeats alternate with intervals of gliding with the wings folded. Shortly before a winter dusk, a downy once sailed low over my head, twittering loudly. It disappeared at what seemed like full speed into a roosting hole in an oak snag. From inside, it bade the woods goodnight with a muffled snicker.

The Perching Birds *(Order Passeriformes)*

BLUE JAY
Cyanocitta cristata

FIELD MARKS: This is our only blue bird with a crest. The back, wings and tail are of iridescent blues with black and white trim. The face is white with a black outline. The bill and feet are black. White is visible in flight on the secondary feathers and outer tail feathers. The sexes are indistinguishable.

LENGTH: 10 inches.

VOICE: The wide vocal range includes raucous screams, flutelike melodies and a near-perfect imitation of the red-tailed hawk.

RANGE IN OUR REGION: Winters and nests throughout.

HABITAT: Usually near tall trees. Especially numerous in residential areas, on farms and in woodlands.

This handsome and brilliantly colored bird is one of the best known and most easily identified in eastern North America. It is the only jay in the eastern United States north of Florida. It is aggressive at the feeders but limits its visits to quick forays. It is also aggressive with larger birds, especially raptors such as hawks and owls, which it mobs noisily. Blue jays are gregarious, feeding and socializing in highly vocal groups. They move to and from roosting areas in loose formations at dawn and dusk.

The blue jay's diet undeniably includes the eggs and the young of smaller birds. However, a much larger portion of its rations is composed of insect pests. The blue jay is one of the few avian controllers of the hairy caterpillars. Other animal prey includes frogs, salamanders, snails, mice and even adult birds as large as hairy woodpeckers. Ironically, the feathers of blue jays killed by hawks and owls are sometimes found in the nesting material of birds the blue jay eats.

Vegetable matter makes up three-quarters of the blue jay's total intake. The bird relied heavily on chestnuts before a man-induced blight wasted the stands of this noble tree. Adaptations to other nuts and to acorns attest to the bird's versatility. Its practice of burying nuts and fruits makes it an important agent in reforestation.

Watching a blue jay gulp whole sunflower seeds at the feeder, you are tempted to conclude that the bird can digest the seeds whole. But like all birds, blue jays have short, weight-saving digestive tracts and can not digest the seed coats. The blue jay flies to a perch, and like those in the snowy scene above, coughs up the seeds from its crop and opens them one at a time by holding them against a limb and striking a single powerful blow with its heavy beak. I can offer no explanation of how the bird is apparently able to swallow a hulled morsel through a crop full of whole seeds.

FAMILY PARIDAE

BLACK-CAPPED CHICKADEE
Parus atricapillus

FIELD MARKS: Similar to the Carolina chickadee (*see* p. 11) except for the narrow whitish edgings on the flight feathers of the wings and tail and the slightly rustier flanks. The sexes are indistinguishable.
LENGTH: 4½ inches.
VOICE: The song consists of a clearly whistled FEE-BEE, the second note a full tone lower than the first. Scolding notes include rasping whistles of CHICK-A-DEE-DEE-DEE and simply DEE-DEE-DEE.
RANGE IN OUR REGION: Nests and winters from Virginia northward. Hybridizes with the Carolina chickadee on the southeastern fringe of its vast breeding range across the northern part of the continent. Expands its range slightly southward in winter. May be seen in the higher mountains of North Carolina in any season.
HABITAT: Woodlands of any type, orchards, suburban shrubbery.

The black-capped chickadee closely resembles the more southerly Carolina chickadee in appearance and ecology. The black-capped is slightly larger and has whiter cheeks and edgings on the primary flight feathers, but these nuances are visible only under scrutiny at close range. A side-by-side comparison of pure-strain black-capped and Carolina chickadees is rarely possible, because the two species intergrade and hybridize where they overlap, principally in Virginia and westward to Ohio. The individual illustrated was photographed at Hawk Mountain, Pennsylvania, which is north of the principal range of overlap. Bearing in mind that birds have wings and can show up as errant visitors almost anywhere, anytime, we are largely safe in identifying as a Carolina any chickadee seen south of Virginia. In Virginia, Maryland and southern Ohio, chickadee identities are sometimes blurred, and finding a hybrid, perhaps one voicing irregular variations of the four-note call of the Carolina or the two-note call of the black-capped, is an opportunity open to the careful observer. In the absence of hybridization, these calls are used more reliably than appearances to make the distinction.

The black-capped, following a tendency of boreal birds to be less wary of humans, is tamer than its southern counterpart and can sometimes be trained to take food from the hand.

CAROLINA CHICKADEE
Parus carolinensis

FIELD MARKS: The black cap and bib are separated by white cheeks. The bill is thin and short. The back is gray, the underparts whitish with faint rusty blushes on the sides. The sexes are indistinguishable.
LENGTH: 4¼ inches.
VOICE: A clearly whistled TSEE-DEE, TSEE-DEE descending a full note at each step.
RANGE IN OUR REGION: Nests and winters throughout. Does not migrate.
HABITAT: Hardwood and pine forests, lawn trees and shrubbery.

The Carolina chickadee is the smallest bird to visit our seed feeders. It is also usually the first to do so after each disturbance; its boldness enables it to compete at the feeder with the larger, more wary birds. The chickadee is even more vocal than its kindred titmouse and is readily summoned with a swishing or kissing sound. In spring the territorial call is easily imitated, and running conversations can be held with successive chickadees as we pass through their nesting territories.

In summer the chickadee's diet consists of small insects, insect larvae and eggs. In cooler months the fare switches to a variety of seeds. *Helianthus*, the Jerusalem artichoke, produces sunflowerlike seeds which are among the Carolina chickadee's favorite natural foods. Chickadees travel the winter woods in small flocks, scurrying like mice through and over the branches. They cling upside down to pinecones, alder cones and sweet gum balls, prying out seeds and perhaps fugitive insects. Chickadees respond readily to offerings of suet and table scraps. I have even seen them flit between crows and vultures to steal tidbits of carrion. The favored fare in winter is sunflower seeds, which the chickadee nabs quickly from feeders laxly guarded by larger birds. Like the titmouse, the chickadee holds its prize against a branch and hammers manfully into the hull to extract the seed. The bird scolds incessantly while feeding.

TUFTED TITMOUSE
Parus bicolor

FIELD MARKS: The crown, back and tail are gray, and the underparts are white. The head is crested. A pinkish blush ornaments the flanks. The sexes are indistinguishable.
LENGTH: 5½ inches.
VOICE: A loud, sharp PEETER-PEETER-PEETER, plus a variety of scolding, chattering notes.
RANGE IN OUR REGION: Winters and nests throughout.
HABITAT: Deciduous woodlands, residential areas.

The "tomtit" grooms the oaks and hickories, picking insects and their eggs from the leaves and twigs. In winter the diet shifts toward small acorns, meaty seeds and the softer fruits available in the leafless woods— wild grapes and the fruit of the strawberry bush and black gum. At the seed feeder the titmouse alights, scolds briefly and departs with a sunflower seed. Holding the seed to a limb with its feet, it hammers open the hull and extracts the meat. When the feeder is empty, the titmouse is the first to complain.

Like its close relative the Carolina chickadee, the tufted titmouse can easily be "swished," or attracted by a simulation of its irritation call. Squeaks and kisslike sounds also draw the bird in close, its crest and voice raised in protest.

The titmouse is with us in all seasons but seems in evidence only during the colder months. Though its bland colors blend with the naked woods, the bird is too vocal in winter to be overlooked. Our presence in the hardwoods sets it to scolding from fifty yards away. Toward spring the harsh notes mellow to the clearly whistled PEETER-PEETER-PEETER of the male's territorial pronouncement. Later, when nesting, the titmouse falls silent, except to decry the presence of a cat, an owl or a snake in the vicinity of its brood.

FAMILY SITTIDAE

WHITE-BREASTED NUTHATCH
Sitta carolinensis

FIELD MARKS: Cap and cape are glossy black on the male, gray on the female. No other head markings are evident. The face and the underparts are white. The back is blue-gray. White shows on the outer tail feathers.
LENGTH: 5 inches.
VOICE: A nasal YANK, YANK.
RANGE IN OUR REGION: Winters and nests throughout.
HABITAT: Hardwood forests, shade trees in residential areas.

Of the world's thirty nuthatches, the white-breasted is the largest. Size, however, costs the bird none of the acrobatic versatility characteristic of nuthatches. In contrast to the brown-headed nuthatch, a bird of the conifers, the white-breasted is usually found in deciduous forests. It utilizes or enlarges small natural openings in the hardwoods for roosting and nesting cavities. It often occupies abandoned excavations of downy woodpeckers.

Pairs of white-breasted nuthatches remain mated year-round. They travel through their feeding territories with groups of other birds of the deciduous woodlands, such as chickadees, titmice, kinglets, creepers and wintering warblers. A pair stays in touch by mischievous undertones of toots and giggles.

Food in warmer months is mostly insects and their larvae captured on twigs or pried from crevices in bark. Seeds, nuts, acorns and hibernating insects comprise the winter diet. With vigorous blows the white-breasted hammers away loose chips of bark to expose wood-boring insects lurking beneath. Sunflower seeds and offerings of beef suet bring the "treemouse" to the feeders for close observation. With patience this forward bird can be coaxed to take food from the hand. Morsels it can not immediately use it stores in crotches of trees and crevices in bark for later consumption. Each visit to the sunflower seed bin is followed either by a stop at a nearby tree where the white-breasted wedges the seed into a crack in the bark and hacks it open, or by a longer trek to a cache.

♂

RED-BREASTED NUTHATCH
Sitta canadensis

FIELD MARKS: The black band through the eye and and the white stripe above it are distinctive. The breast is rusty cinnamon, the upperparts slate blue, and the cap black. The sexes are indistinguishable.
LENGTH: 4 inches.
VOICE: Nasal AANK, AANK similar to but higher than the white-breasted's notes.
RANGE IN OUR REGION: Winters irregularly throughout; nests in highest Appalachians.
HABITAT: Coniferous woods.

The red-breasted nuthatch visits in winter from its nesting grounds in the northern coniferous forests. A small population that nests in the higher mountains of our region has only to move eastward a hundred miles to find suitable wintering conditions. The red-breasted's arrival is unpredictable; it may be abundant in the piedmont and coastal plain in some winters, absent in others. It winters most predictably in the mountains and toward the northern parts of our region.

The bird is almost always seen in conifers, where it specializes in extracting seeds from the cones. Pine and spruce are favored. Single birds or small groups of red-breasteds often mix with pine warblers and brown creepers, the nuthatches keeping to the higher parts of the pines and sociably exchanging their tinny nasal notes. The majority of sightings are made by scrutinizing these flocks with binoculars. The black stripe through the eye and the white stripe above it provide clear diagnostic markings. Deep, bouncing undulations define the flight profile.

"Busiest" of our nuthatches, the red-breasted is constantly in motion, scouring the boles, branches and needles, and assuming, like all nuthatches, a variety of upside-down positions in its search. Quick flights to intercept flying insects interrupt the mouselike movements over the trees' surfaces. The nesting cavities of red-breasted nuthatches are identified by smudges of pine sap around the opening.

Ed Burroughs

BROWN-HEADED NUTHATCH
Sitta pusilla

FIELD MARKS: The body is short and stubby. The tail does not extend past the wing tips at rest. The brown cap is interrupted by a white crescent at the nape. The back is gray, the underparts whitish. The sexes are indistinguishable.

LENGTH: 3½ inches.

VOICE: Mouselike squeaks.

RANGE IN OUR REGION: Winters and nests east of the mountains, principally in the piedmont, sandhills and coastal plain.

HABITAT: Pine forests and savannahs.

The brown-headed is the smallest eastern nuthatch. It is closely associated with the southern pine forests. A great American birder, Frank Chapman, wrote: "This little nuthatch, the red-cockaded woodpecker, and the pine warbler are the characteristic birds of the great pineries in the southern states. Frequently they are found associated. The nuthatches . . . are talkative little sprites . . . each one chatters away without paying the slightest attention to what his companions are saying."

The brown-headed grooms the piney spires from crown to stump. Like other nuthatches, it is as comfortable in head-down postures as it is upright. It assumes every conceivable angle and position during its foragings: it may circle a branch headfirst, pry into a cone from a sideways stance, or run headlong down the trunk to capture a falling morsel.

Pine seeds are important in the brown-headed nuthatch's diet, but it is always on the lookout for insects. It is a major controller of the moths whose larvae attack growing stands of pine. As such, the brown-headed does man a significant economic service. Ants and other insects that feed on the sap-weeping pine wounds also figure in the brown-headed's fare. Feeding flocks converse in a soft prattle of BIT, BIT syllables intensifying as the group takes flight. When alarmed, the brown-headed nuthatch sometimes takes the same defense as the brown creeper; it freezes against the bark and waits motionless for the danger to pass.

CAROLINA WREN
Thryothorus ludovicianus

FIELD MARKS: A white eye stripe runs the length of the head. Upperparts are rufous; underparts are buff. The tail is held erect. The sexes are indistinguishable.
LENGTH: 4¾ inches.
VOICE: Astonishingly loud, clear triplets TEA-KETTLE, TEA-KETTLE, TEA-KETTLE often followed by a rattle.
RANGE IN OUR REGION: Winters and nests throughout.
HABITAT: Found near the ground in fencerows and thick underbrush.

This is the largest eastern wren and one of our most vocal birds. That so much noise could be made by such a small creature takes some getting used to. At close range the volume and clarity of its voice, bursting from a briar thicket, can be startling. A Carolina wren once awakened me from an afternoon nap by singing its explosive notes from a lampshade on my bedside table. The awakening was, to say the least, traumatic.

The bird is also very inquisitive. My visitor had entered the house through an open door, as Carolina wrens often do, to explore the premises. This curiosity often results in their being trapped in homes and having to be escorted out. They frequently consider the attics, porches, garages and crawl spaces beneath our houses to be legitimate foraging grounds. Sadly, I once caught one in a mousetrap in my cellar. I still have no idea how it got in. Invading our privacy on winter foraging trips, Carolina wrens mark nesting spots for later use in and around our homes. I have found them nesting in hanging planters and coat pockets on the porch, as well as in more conventional sites such as eaves and mailboxes. During my lunch hour, one enterprising pair nearly completed a nest on the engine of my tractor, which I had left in the field.

Because I have probably had more personal experience with the Carolina wren than with any other bird, I conclude that it is our most personable. To this cheery songster human civilization has been a boon. Humans benefit too from the Carolina wren's ceaseless attack on soft-bodied caterpillars during the nesting season. In winter the natural diet switches to such persistent fruits as poke and honeysuckle berries and to ants and hibernating spiders. Winter hunger makes the birds even more forward than they are in summer, and they probe offerings of suet and a mixture of cornmeal, bacon drippings and peanut butter. Once our namesake wren develops a taste for this mixture, it will gobble it eagerly from a patient hand.

FAMILY MIMIDAE

MOCKINGBIRD
Mimus polyglottos

FIELD MARKS: The crown and back are gray, the wings and tail a darker gray. The tail is long and active. White is visible in the outer tail and wings at rest, conspicuously so in flight. The sexes are indistinguishable.
LENGTH: 9 inches.
VOICE: Virtually limitless. Astonishing tonal range and variety. Irritation call a cross CHAK.
RANGE IN OUR REGION: Nests and winters throughout.
HABITAT: Open country, fencerows, lawn shrubbery.

Perhaps only the European skylark is as renowned as the mockingbird for its vocalizations. The mocker can imitate almost any sound it hears: the squeak of a gate hinge, the meow of a cat, the cry of a human infant. It can effectively echo the call of a tanager, upon hearing it, and, without pausing, render an accurate chime of an evening grosbeak that it hasn't heard in several months. I have heard a mockingbird mock a blue jay that was mocking a red-tailed hawk.

Imitation is not the only source of inspiration for the mockingbird. The bird can compose endless melodic passages, usually in short phrases repeated a few times. The mocker may sit for long periods on an exposed perch such as a TV antenna, interjecting mockeries into its stream of composition, and finally take flight without interrupting its song.

The mockingbird mimics the appearance of the loggerhead shrike, the "butcherbird." This may account for the mocker's aggressive demeanor with other birds; its resemblance to the shrike may give it a power base beyond what its own weak bill could sustain. Flashing with slow, rowing wingbeats the conspicuous white markings in its wings, the mocker cantankerously drives other birds from the seed feeder, though it can not eat the seeds. The shrike shows similar markings but has a faster wingbeat.

The natural food in winter is mostly the persistent fruits of honeysuckle, holly and poke, and insects when available. It relishes raisins and table scraps.

Formerly a bird of the southeast, the mocker for some years has been extending its range northward, probably because of a beneficial relationship with man.

EASTERN BLUEBIRD
Sialia sialis

FIELD MARKS: The male has brilliant blue upperparts. The female is a dusky gray or brown with blue in the wings and tail. Both sexes have a rusty throat and breast and white lower underparts. They sit perched with slightly hunched shoulders.
LENGTH: 5½ inches.
VOICE: A sweet, slurred warble, CHER-WEET.
RANGE IN OUR REGION: Winters in all localities except higher mountains. Nests throughout.
HABITAT: Sits on open perches along roadsides, in farmyards and in orchards.

♂

The small size and the uncrested head of the bluebird easily distinguish it from the blue jay, the only other bluish bird wintering in our region. Confused identities are more likely in warmer months, when indigo buntings and blue grosbeaks join the bluebirds nesting in our region. The bluebird's diagnostic marking is the rusty band across the chest and down the side, possessed by no other blue bird in our region in any season.

The bluebird's soft, cheerful notes beckon us to the window on a winter day. The male's deep blue cloak and rusty sash brighten the dooryard as he hovers before alighting at the feeder. His slightly less colorful lady joins him, and the two move from perch to feeder, gently winging the air with the grace and charm of ballet performers.

The bluebird is principally an insect eater the year round. It hunts from an exposed perch, dropping down to nab unwary insects. Sometimes the downward swoop is interrupted by a tentative hovering while the bird watches the movements of its prey. The bluebird makes some lateral forays to catch insects on the wing.

The bluebird nests in abandoned woodpecker holes and other natural cavities, and readily accepts man-made nesting boxes. But civilization has been a mixed blessing to the bluebird, since it has brought with it not only birdhouses but humanity's near-parasites, the

English sparrow and the starling. These pernicious aliens have all but eliminated the bluebird in some areas by usurping its nesting spaces. The celebrated naturalist John Terres, who worked with bluebirds in North Carolina, suggests that if the entrance to a nesting box is one inch in diameter, it will permit the bluebird to enter, yet will exclude the sparrow. Also, the bluebird will occupy a box placed as low as four feet off the ground, a height which discourages competition. Warning: Snake guards are an absolute necessity, for snakes frequently climb the post, enter the box and eat the eggs, young and adults.

Missouri and New York hail the bluebird as state bird. Youth organizations and conservation groups have undertaken ambitious projects to provide nesting boxes for the bluebird. With its quiet, gentle beauty, the bluebird appeals to the quiet, gentle elements of human nature and easily captures our protective sympathies. The bluebird eagerly accepts offerings of cornmeal, bacon fat and peanut butter in winter and the nesting shelters we provide in springtime. It needs both in order to survive the assaults of the starlings and English sparrows introduced into its habitat.

FAMILY SYLVIIDAE

RUBY-CROWNED KINGLET
Regulus calendula

FIELD MARKS: A tiny, teardrop-shaped bird. Upperparts are olive-drab, underparts light gray. Both sexes show a white eye ring and wing bars. The male displays a glowing red crown when irritated.
LENGTH: 3½ inches.
VOICE: A short, gritty, scolding ZIT, ZIT. The rich, melodious breeding song is not heard in our region.
RANGE IN OUR REGION: Present only during winter; avoids higher mountain elevations.
HABITAT: Seen in virtually all woodland and shrubby habitats, including lawn shrubbery.

♂

Because the ruby-crowned kinglet has no noticeable coloration, the very small size and teardrop shape best identify the bird. When agitated, usually by the presence of another male, the male erects a crimson crest which approaches luminescence. Two males sparring in a shrub across a lawn appear as gyrating Christmas lights, their positions easily marked by the brilliant crests. When the encounter ends, the crests are completely concealed, and the drab brown bodies blend with winter's wind-tossed detritus. Females and males not in combat are identified by white wing bars and white rings around their eyes. The rings are broken at the top and set the beady dark eyes in stark relief. The bird carries an intent, staring facial expression.

The ruby-crowned travels in small feeding flocks often mixing with golden-crowneds. (*See* p. 73.) Often a flock of kinglets will be joined by a single brown creeper who moves upward on the tree trunks while the kinglets flit nervously in the branches. The ruby-crowneds more frequently feed in the lower branches while the golden-crowneds scour the upper twigs. However, the two may mix at all heights.

Kinglets are constantly in motion. Photographing them is very difficult, for they are rarely in one place for a full second. The ruby-crowned seems slightly the more nervous, its wings flicking out continually, its body zigzagging in short leaps and erratic swooping flights.

I have seen only the ruby-crowned at my offerings of bacon fat, cornmeal and peanut butter. The birds often hover as they pick at the mixture and as they feed higher in the trees. Natural food consists of tiny insects picked from the twigs of shrubs and deciduous trees, and from needles and cones of conifers.

FAMILY STURNIDAE

STARLING
Sturnus vulgaris

FIELD MARKS: The long, pointed bill, hunched posture, short tail and short, pointed wings define the starling's silhouette. In winter the plumage is speckled and the bill is dark. A spring molt changes the plumage to a more uniform glossy black with brown edgings on the back and wings and purple iridescence below. The bill becomes yellow in spring. The sexes are indistinguishable.
LENGTH: 6 inches.
VOICE: Cacophonous squeaks and whirring noises.
RANGE IN OUR REGION: Winters and nests in all sections.
HABITAT: Virtually all habitats occupied by man. Abundant on farms and in cities.

The honeysuckle, *Lonicera japonica*, is a rare and venerated ornamental plant in its native Japanese range. Introduced into North America to stabilize railroad embankments, the honeysuckle proliferated in the absence of its native restrictions, choking and altering the landscape. So, too, did the alien starling. One hundred starlings released in New York City in 1890 multiplied unchecked until the species is now one of the most numerous on the continent. Only the red-winged blackbird may outnumber the starling, who nests in every available shelter near civilization in the warmer months and ravages the countryside in endless feeding flocks in winter. Food is obtained from a wide variety of plant and animal sources.

Since there are few native birds adapted to life in the heart of major cities, the starling's occupancy, along with its fellow aliens, the English sparrow and the European rock dove (domestic pigeon), displaces few native species. To most urban dwellers, these three species *are* the available birdlife, and their control over the habitat is unlamented. In fact, the starling does not limit its distressing presence to the urban center, but usurps the suburbs and farmlands as well. The impact on the legitimate native birds and on mankind has been unfortunate, to say the least. Only the wilderness areas, devoid of man and his buildings, have been spared the starling's invasion.

The starling is a bird who nests in cavities and visits his messy nidifications most often upon his principal benefactor, man. The same host provides most of the starling's food in the form of a continent-wide banquet of livestock feeder lots, garbage dumps, growing crops and untidy streets. The results of this bird's presence are very often costly to the farmer, the taxpayer and the homeowner.

The naturalist observes the starling's ingress from another point of view, seeing a native birdlife and a continent's life system badly dislocated by an aggressive, prolific alien. In all habitats the starling usurps the feeding and nesting places of the native birds. In farming country much larger populations of doves, killdeer and meadowlarks might be sustained if the hordes of starlings were absent. Highly valued cavity-nesting birds such as bluebirds, crested flycatchers and purple martins suffer reproductive failures as starlings, with the not-infrequent help of English sparrows, evict them from their natural and man-made shelters. Alarmingly, starlings are invading the woodlands and evicting from their excavations woodpeckers as large as the mighty pileated. The starling's approach to commandeering the home of a larger and stronger bird is one of tenacious harassment which makes it impossible for the owner to carry on its domestic functions.

The starling subtly phased itself into the North American life scheme, and while two or three human generations took little notice, the alien displaced many native birds. Solutions to the problem of controlling the population of starlings are conceived more successfully than they are applied, for natural controls are the only effective long-term limits. At one time, urban-nesting peregrine falcons provided token control. Sharp-shinned hawks still take a few starlings from parks and residential areas, but the starling has few natural controls other than disease and the limits to its food supply. One wildlife manager suggested, only partially in jest, that a hunting season be set for the starling, with very strict bag limits which are certain to be exceeded.

FAMILY PARULIDAE

YELLOW-RUMPED WARBLER
(Formerly Myrtle Warbler)
Dendroica coronata

FIELD MARKS: Both sexes have a yellow rump, crown and side patches. The throat and eye rings are white; the back is blue-gray. The female is duller, brownish.
LENGTH: 4¾ inches.
VOICE: The bird is not noted for its song. A CHEK note can be heard during winter feeding.
RANGE IN OUR REGION: Winters in piedmont and coastal plain.
HABITAT: Found in most trees and shrubs inland; abundant in coastal shrubs.

The yellow-rumped is our most common wintering warbler. Upland during cold months, it is easily found in pine and deciduous woods and in yard shrubs. Along the coast, the bird winters in great numbers and passes north and south in vast migrating flocks. As many as twenty-four thousand have been observed along the South Carolina coast in a four-hour period during the spring migration.

The bird has been called "myrtle warbler" for its delight in the fruit of the wax myrtle or bayberry bush. Successive freezes make the gray clusters of bayberries more irresistible to the myrtle warbler. In winter hardly a wax myrtle can be found along the coast unattended by its namesake warbler. Winter food also includes insects; the myrtle frequently visits the sapsucker's wells to drink the sap and to eat the insects attracted to it. The myrtle can, when necessary, switch from insects and its favored berries to a diet composed largely of seeds, but it does not visit our seed feeders. Along with the kinglets and the bluebirds, it relishes a mixture of cornmeal, bacon fat and peanut butter.

The yellow-rumped does not nest in our region, but it is a common migrant and wintering species. When we see it in the fall and early winter, the plumage is somewhat subdued, although the diagnostic white throat and the yellow rump and side patches are always part of the male's attire. The photograph shows a male in January. Toward spring the male dons his vivid blacks and blues; the brilliant yellows flash in the greening branches as the yellow-rumped chases insects along the migration route to nesting grounds in the far north.

PINE WARBLER
Dendroica pinus

FIELD MARKS: The lack of markings on the back is an important feature. Wing bars are prominent, and the underparts have varying amounts of yellow extending farther rearward on the male than on the female. There is a faint eye stripe.

LENGTH: 4¾ inches.

VOICE: Short, faint notes on winter feeding grounds. The territorial song is a high, piping SI-SI-SI-SI-SI delivered with such physical commitment that one observer noted, "Why, all of the bird sings."*

RANGE IN OUR REGION: Winters and nests in all regions east of the mountains. Quits higher, colder areas in winter.

HABITAT: Pines and other conifers.

* L. A. Hausman, *Field Book of Eastern Birds.* New York: G. P. Putnam's Sons, 1946. Hausman does not give the source of this quote.

None of our birds has a name more aptly describing its habitat and life style. The pine warbler is almost always found in coniferous trees, mostly pines. Experienced birders differentiate the pine from other warblers it closely resembles by the type of tree in which it is found. Smudges of pine sap on the bird's feathers often attest to its fondness for these trees.

During summer and during the migration periods, the pine can be mistaken for any of several of the plain-backed warblers. During winter, however, most warblers leave the Carolinas. The pine is our only unstreaked wintering warbler with wing bars.

The habit of hitching like a creeper up and down pine trunks and along branches gives the pine warbler one of its nicknames, "pine creeper." It scours the bark and needles for spiders and insects and helps itself to pine seeds when they are available. Wild berries augment the winter diet. It relishes a mixture of cornmeal, bacon fat and peanut butter.

FAMILY PLOCEIDAE

ENGLISH (OR HOUSE) SPARROW
Passer domesticus

FIELD MARKS: A stout, conical bill and short legs separate this species from the true sparrows. The male has a gray cap, white cheeks and a black bib covering the throat and upper breast. The back and wings are chestnut and brown, and the underparts are an unstreaked, dingy white. The female lacks the bib, the gray cap and the chestnut hues and is generally duller.
LENGTH: 5¼ inches.
VOICE: Monotonous, unmusical CHEEPs.
RANGE IN OUR REGION: Winters and nests throughout.
HABITAT: Cities, suburbs, commercial structures, barns; never far from buildings.

The National Geographic Society, in *Song and Garden Birds of North America*, describes the English sparrow as a "cocky street gamin and barnyard brawler." Whenever humans construct their buildings, the house sparrow moves in a messy heap of nesting debris and cheeps from the eaves a monotonous litany. In North America the bird is completely dependent upon man and is virtually never out of sight of a human settlement. Food is a variety of seeds, insects and refuse often provided by human enterprise. It was with the English sparrow in mind that someone coined the saying, "Two can live as cheaply as one if one is a horse and the other a sparrow."

Beginning in 1850 a series of attempts were made to establish this Old World weaver finch (it is not a true sparrow) as a North American resident. English immigrants wished to have the bird present to remind them of their homeland. The first attempts failed, but the results of later releases were far more successful than desirable. The English sparrow is pugnacious and prolific. Its success has been at the expense of people, including those of English extraction, and very much to the detriment of the native birds. The eastern bluebird has suffered most severely from the house sparrow's invasion. The alien finch usurps the bluebird's nesting spaces in trees and birdhouses so aggressively that the bluebird has been extirpated in some localities and is numerically reduced in most. Placing a nesting box at a height of four feet and making the opening exactly one inch in diameter admits the bluebird and excludes the English sparrow. (See p. 19.)

♂

FAMILY ICTERIDAE

BROWN-HEADED COWBIRD
Molothrus ater

FIELD MARKS: The male has a glossy black body and a uniform chocolate brown head. The female is a plain mouse gray. The bill is shorter and heavier than in other wintering icterids.
LENGTH: 6½ inches.
VOICE: On winter feeding grounds a soft, rich CHUCK. Breeding song is a three-note squeak probably pleasing only to a female brown-headed cowbird: KLICK, TSI-EEE.
RANGE IN OUR REGION: Breeds and winters throughout.
HABITAT: Pastures, usually near livestock.

The term "breeds" instead of "nests" applies to the brown-headed cowbird because it does not build a nest or care for its own young. The female, after a promiscuous courtship with the group of males with whom she spends the spring, deposits her eggs in the nest of some more diligent parent. The brown-headed, the only eastern cowbird, parasitizes the nests of over two hundred species of birds, usually favoring vireos, warblers, flycatchers and sparrows as foster parents.

The cowbird is equally pesky at the seed feeder, typically scattering birds as large as cardinals to dominate the pickings.

The plumage does not appear to change with the seasons. The female is the only plain grayish brown bird in our region with a sharp conical bill. The male's black head and brown body are diagnostic. Both sexes hold the tail high when perched.

The cowbird's name suggests how it gains its livelihood. It is a native North American bird associated ecologically with grazing ungulates. It captures insects flushed from the grass by livestock and picks others from their backs; hence the folk name "tick bird." It often travels in flocks with starlings, picking in livestock droppings. Almost any aspect of the cowbird's life style tempts us to be judgmental and subjective, yet natural order rewards the cowbird's promiscuity, parental negligence and coprophagy.

♂

CARDINAL
Cardinalis cardinalis
(Formerly *Richmondena cardinalis*)

FIELD MARKS: The male's plumage is a uniform brilliant red except for a black facial mask which appears square when seen head on. The bill is red. The female wears rusty brown on her head, back and underparts, but has redder wings and tail. Both sexes sport crests which can be raised or lowered.

LENGTH: 7¾ inches.

VOICE: The agitation call and feeding notes heard in winter are brief CHIPs. The male's territorial call is a clear, loudly whistled series of quickening tempo, WHOIT-WHOIT-WHOIT-WHAT CHEER, WHAT CHEER.

RANGE IN OUR REGION: Nests and winters throughout.

HABITAT: Underbrush of woodlots, shrubbery and lawn trees, brush thickets in open spaces.

Of the "redbird" Audubon declared: "In richness of plumage, elegance of motion and strength of song, this species surpasses all its kindred in the United States." The citizens of North Carolina, Virginia, West Virginia, Kentucky, Illinois, Indiana and Ohio agreed and selected the cardinal as their state bird.

Indeed, the cardinal's unique brilliance suggests a tropical setting more than a wintry scene in the Carolinas. With its pointed crest and dazzling crimson plumage, the male cardinal is unlike any other bird in eastern North America. Only the summer tanager, in its season, can be mistaken for the cardinal. In a winter snowstorm the birds puff up their feathers for insulation, and the reds in both sexes sometimes take on a rosy pinkish hue, probably reflecting the blues in the subdued light. It is a phenomenon worth watching for.

Cardinals are thought to mate for life. Even in midwinter when natural food is scarcest and when, in most species, it's every bird for him- or herself, the cardinal's lady follows him closely. Toward spring the bond strengthens, and the pair feeds and sings together. Unlike the females of most species of birds, to whom

♂

♀   ♂

nature has given no part in the territorial statement, the female cardinal sings as beautifully as her mate, though more softly.

Audubon, speaking principally of the male, noted: "During the love season, the song is emitted with increased emphasis by this proud musician, who, as if aware of his power, swells his throat, spreads his rosy tail, droops his wings, and leans alternately to the right and left, as if on the eve of his expiring with delight at the delicious sounds of his own voice."

In summer both sexes feed the nestlings large insects including beetles and grasshoppers. One of my favorite reference books on birds contains an extraor-

dinary picture of a male cardinal so consumed with the instinctive urge to feed young pink things that he is feeding insects to goldfish in a garden pool! Winter fare, as in most fringillids, turns mainly to seeds. The seeds of grasses and legumes are included in the diet. The size of the bird and proportionate strength of the heavy seed-cracking bill indicate that it is able to handle those seeds with the tougher coats. At the feeder, cardinals seem to relish the cereal grains such as millet and milo about equally with sunflower seeds. They show a preference for feeding on the ground over taking seed directly from the station.

EVENING GROSBEAK
Hesperiphona vespertina

FIELD MARKS: The male has unmistakable brilliant yellow back and underparts, black tail and primary feathers, and white secondaries appearing as a white patch on the back at rest. There is a yellow-brown stripe above the eye. The female's colors are duller, with white occurring arbitrarily in the wings and tail, though the color pattern is basically similar to that of the male.

LENGTH: 7½ inches.

VOICE: A chimed Q.

RANGE IN OUR REGION: Winters unpredictably in all sections.

HABITAT: Deciduous and coniferous woods while wintering in our region; conifers for nesting.

An early American observer somehow concluded that the evening grosbeak inhabits "dark retreats, and leaves them only at the approach of midnight" and was therefore a bird of the evening. It is a quaint thought, but the result is a misnomer. The "hawfinch" is very much a diurnal bird, flashing its black and white and gold in the winter sun.

But "grosbeak" is no misnomer. This bird's massive, straw-colored bill is perhaps the most efficient seed-cracking instrument in all of nature. We are safe in asserting, at least, that the evening grosbeak has the strongest jaws of any fringillid in our region—they are said to be able to crack a cherry pit. In view of the escalating price of sunflower seed, a flock of evening grosbeaks can rapidly consume an expensive meal at the feeder. They travel and dine in flocks of up to forty birds, shuttling from nearby perches to the feeder and squabbling over the fare. Once a grosbeak claims a feeding spot, it may sit for several minutes fighting off its fellows and shelling numerous seeds.

The flight is undulating but direct. Both sexes show conspicuous white in the wings in flight and join in announcing the approach of a feeding flock with clear, delicately chimed notes. The scientific name, *Hesperiphona vespertina*, is related to the Greek name for Hesperia, "the land to the west," and to Hesperos, the evening star. Originally, the evening grosbeak was a bird of the American west, ranging from Mexico to central Canada. In 1890 the first grosbeaks visited New

♂

England, gladdening that winter-numbed region with their song and colors. Since then the bird has continued to expand its wintering and nesting ranges eastward, with the nesting range centered around the Great Lakes. In winter the eastern populations move southward *and northward* from the nesting corridor, their seasonal movements more aptly described as wanderings than as disciplined migrations. One can hardly resist speculating that the general expansion is at least partly due to human generosity.

♀

♂

PURPLE FINCH
Carpodacus purpureus

FIELD MARKS: The male's uniform raspberry upperparts and breast are diagnostic. The heavily streaked, brownish female is distinguished from sparrows by the heavier conical bill and white head markings. Both sexes have a deeply notched tail.
LENGTH: 6 inches.
VOICE: On winter feeding grounds, a sharp musical TINK, intensifying as the flock takes flight.
RANGE IN OUR REGION: Winters in all sections.
HABITAT: Deciduous and coniferous woodlands.

From a distance a group of purple finches feeding in a conifer look like oversized raspberries. The male's coloration appears roughly uniform above, looking, according to the official National Geographic Society description, "like a large-billed sparrow that has been dipped in red wine." The female is sparrow brown above with streaked underparts. Both sexes have deeply notched tails and erectile feathers on the crest and nape.

Until a few years ago there would have been no bird in our region with which the purple finch could be confused. Now, however, the closely similar house finch winters with us, occasionally feeding in mixed flocks with the purple. The more localized color of the male house finch and the darker and more uniform brown of the female house finch distinguish them from the purple finch.

The purple finch is very much a winter bird in the Carolinas and nearby states. It arrives usually around Thanksgiving and departs in early spring, following the freezing nights northward to its nesting grounds in the Canadian conifers. While wintering with us it enjoys a natural diet of weed and grass seeds as well as the seeds of sweet gum and tulip "poplar." On a bright winter day I once saw a flock of purple finches join a group of goldfinches feeding in a sweet gum tree. Nearly all the spiny seedballs toward the top of the tree had clinging to them a finch, colored yellow-green or raspberry or brown. Against the cloudless blue sky they looked like Christmas ornaments dangling in the sweet gum's winter-bare crown. I saw on another occasion purple finches' colors contrast with those of a company of evening grosbeaks high in the spire of a tulip tree. Both species were systematically breaking the individual samaras from the artichokelike fruit structures and pinching off the seeds. The dry leaves beneath the tulip tree crackled as the debris rained down.

Purple finches often perch quietly for sustained periods, waiting in a tree near a sunflower seed feeder for the auspicious moment to begin a communal "feed." When the feast begins, the composed behavior degenerates into a sexist squabble as the females drive the males from the feeder, then haggle among themselves over the fare. The males sit patiently in the shrubs nearby, venturing to the sunflower seeds only after the edge is off the ladies' hunger. Eventually, all occupy a spot at the feeder and sit for long intervals casually hulling the seeds.

♀ purple finch   house finch ♀

♂

♂ purple finch   house finch ♂

HOUSE FINCH
Carpodacus mexicanus

FIELD MARKS: The male's red is localized on the cap, breast and rump. The back, wings and tail of the male are brown; his underparts are streaked with brown. The female is a nearly uniform dark brown. On both sexes the tail is slightly notched.
LENGTH: 5¼ inches.
VOICE: Harsh chatterings; musical finchlike notes.
RANGE IN OUR REGION: Winters sporadically in all sections.
HABITAT: Urban and suburban areas.

The house finch is a native North American bird, but until recently the Rocky Mountains marked the eastern limits of its range. Human intervention broadened the house finch's horizons in 1940 when dealers began shipping the "Hollywood" finches to New York for sale as cage birds. Enough escaped or were released to establish an eastern breeding population. It is interesting that the eastern population shows strong seasonal migratory behavior, whereas western house finches are recorded as sedentary.

As the name suggests, house finches gravitate to human structures. They compete successfully with the English (or house) sparrow for nesting sites and food in urban areas. The bird is steadily expanding its eastern range, radiating as a wintering and nesting species from its original enclave around New York City. Each year it is seen in eastern cities in which it was not previously recorded, and any written material (including this book) describing its eastern range is out of date before it goes to print. As of 1975, the most southerly nesting record in the east was Delaware, though individuals and pairs were sighted in several North Carolina cities in July of that year. It seems probable that a Carolina nesting may be noted in the next few years. That observation could be the good fortune of any alert urban naturalist.

The house finch is easily confused with the purple finch, but they are distinguishable with experience. The male house finch's coloration is closer to red than to raspberry and is localized on the head, breast and rump. The purple's wine hues are more evenly diffused over the upperparts. Males of both species wait until the second year to wear their full colors. The female house finch is grayer and her head markings are less distinct than those of the female purple finch.

Ripening fruit, including commercial crops, provides much of the summer diet. Seeds and berries are important to the house finch in winter. While the bird is an efficient urban scavenger, it dines comfortably on millet and sunflower seeds at the feeder.

♂

PINE SISKIN
Spinus pinus

FIELD MARKS: The upperparts and breast are finely streaked with brown. The bill is long, thin and sharp. Varying amounts of yellow show in the wings and at the base of the deeply notched tail. The males usually show more yellow than the females.

LENGTH: 4¼ inches.

VOICE: Sings in flight, much like the goldfinch, a high descending PIT-TI-TI, PIT-TI-TI. Feeding notes are musical buzzing ZHEEEs.

RANGE IN OUR REGION: Winters irregularly in the northern and mountainous parts of our region.

HABITAT: Prefers conifers, but may be seen in almost any vegetation.

On the wintering grounds, siskins are never seen alone but wander in small flocks through the northern and mountainous parts of our region. They visit one locality or habitat no more predictably than another beyond showing a general preference for conifers. Moreover, their nesting range and even the time of their breeding period varies widely. We are fortunate to have the pine siskin in parts of our region during some winters, but we can not rely on the visits.

When siskins are in the vicinity of humans, however, they are friendly. They feed lustily on sunflower seeds at the feeder and may be so bold as to perch upon their human hosts. A wintering flock in Massachusetts took to waking up their benefactor, if the feeder was empty, by entering his bedroom window and nipping his nose.

Siskins share with their congeners, the goldfinches, a bouncing flight profile. Both species sing in flight, uttering the notes at the moments the wings are flapping. The ascending notes given while feeding and the flight calls are similar in the two species, with those of the siskin being the lower and huskier.

Feeding flocks of siskins stick closely together. I once spent a few minutes watching a group that was interested in some item of food at the shoulder of a road. Each time a car passed, the flock took flight, circling and gyrating in a tight cloud before returning to feed. Flocks of siskins sometimes mix with goldfinches and offer a challenge to the naturalist's ability to distinguish the voices of the two species.

An interesting quirk of the siskin is its weakness for salt. "A flock of siskins," according to Arthur A. Allen, "may suddenly swoop down to cluster around a salt lick or raid a dock area where fish are cured."

♀

AMERICAN GOLDFINCH
Spinus tristis

FIELD MARKS: The winter plumage is pale olive-yellow with white wing bars against black wings and white edging in the primary feathers. Juveniles and adults of both sexes have a roughly similar appearance in winter. By spring the male wears brilliant lemon yellow everywhere except for jet black wings, tail and forehead.

LENGTH: 4¼ inches.

VOICE: The mating song is a high, lengthy warble, sometimes sad but always sweet. The flight song given in all seasons synchronizes a PER-CHIK-O-REE cadence with bursts of wingbeats.

RANGE IN OUR REGION: Nests in the uplands; winters in all sections.

HABITAT: Favors open country in summer; keeps more to woods in winter.

This is the "wild canary," a jaunty bird in its summer brilliance, who wears a drab disguise in winter. So completely different are the winter and breeding plumages that early Americans mistook the winter goldfinch for a separate species.

The goldfinch eats insects such as grubs, hairless caterpillars and grasshoppers in spring and early summer. In all other seasons it is a seed eater. Winter finds the goldfinch prying seeds from the tiny cones of the tag alder or hanging on a geodesic seed globe in a sweet gum tree. Measuring just over four inches, the "yellowbird" may appear no larger than an insect as it picks the individual samaras from the cones high in a tulip tree's crown.

The goldfinch is a late nester. After the spring insect feast it feeds for a while on elm and maple seeds as they ripen. Toward midsummer the seeds of chickory, mullein, dandelion and goldenrod become available. Finally the thistles come into season. Plunging from

winter ♂

summer ♂

its roller-coaster flight, the little wild canary tears at the thistledown, eating the attached seeds and using the down as lining for its nest. The male cares dotingly for his mate during incubation, serving her regurgitated seeds and singing the territorial love song. When the young are born, both parents feed them partially digested seeds as they develop and after they fledge. It is a touching experience to see a feeding family of American goldfinches, as Audubon saw them, in a thistle-dotted pasture. In response to the young's cry for food, a demure sighing whistle strongly contrasting with the demanding CHEEPs of the young of other species, the adults grapple with the ripening thistle heads. Tearing into the urn-shaped seedpods, the goldfinch fills the air with a flurry of thistledown. The autumn wind takes some of the seeds for planting, and the "thistlebird" feeds the rest to his brood.

RUFOUS-SIDED TOWHEE
Pipilo erythrophthalmus

FIELD MARKS: The male's head, bib, neck, back and upper tail are black; the same parts are brown on the female. A broad, rufous stripe runs down the sides; the underbelly is white. White is visible in the wings and tail at rest and in flight. Both sexes have red eyes. A race in the southern part of our region substitutes white for the characteristic red iris.

LENGTH: 7¼ inches.

VOICE: In warmer months, the male sings TOW HEE-EE-EE and DRINK YOUR TEA-EE-EE.

RANGE IN OUR REGION: Winters and nests throughout.

HABITAT: Brush, hedgerows and margins of woods.

The towhee is as dedicated a ground feeder as the quail or the turkey. It scratches mightily in the leaves, raking backward with both feet like a chicken, then leans forward to see what the effort has revealed. I have seen a Carolina wren picking carefully in the wake of a towhee's scratchings for insects the larger bird overlooked. Food includes beetles, pill boxes, centipedes, insects in forest litter, nuts and seeds. At the feeding station, towhees almost never mount the feeder but feed on the ground on seed spilled by other birds. In earlier years, the towhee was suspected of stealing newly sprouted corn and for some years was subjected to open-season shooting. Now under full protection as a songbird, the towhee must contend only with snakes and other natural predators. The cowbird parasitizes towhee nests mercilessly; one nest was found containing eight cowbird eggs, which the owners then struggled to raise.

The singing male takes his vocalizing seriously. I remember working in my vegetable garden during the heat of a summer afternoon, when a noisy towhee flew to a nearby low perch, as they often do, and chattered away. Sweating profusely, I gradually became aware of his instructive song: "Drink your tea-ee-ee!" and retired to the hammock with a glass of the suggested beverage.

Towhees are migratory, and the individuals who winter with us do not necessarily nest in our region. The birds migrate at night, singly or in small family groups.

♀ ♂

DARK-EYED JUNCO, SLATE-COLORED RACE
(Formerly Slate-colored Junco)
Junco hyemalis hyemalis

FIELD MARKS: The junco is identified by uniform slate gray upperparts, white lower belly and outer tail feathers, flesh-colored bill and dark legs. The gray of the female is tinged with brown. Immature birds sometimes appear more brown than gray.

LENGTH: 5¼ inches.

VOICE: Winter notes are sharp TIT-IT-ITs suggesting thin ice cracking on a pond.

RANGE IN OUR REGION: Winters throughout; nests in mountains south to Georgia.

HABITAT: In winter, weedy fields, hedgerows, roadsides and edges of woods.

This is the "snowbird," the only junco in our region. To most people in the lower forty-eight states, its approximate wintering range, the slate-colored junco is winged winter. Its seasonal movements follow close on the heels of the coldest weather. The junco arrives late in autumn and decamps in early spring for subarctic and highland nesting grounds. Wintering with us, juncos can sometimes be seen taking baths in powdery snow, fluttering and dusting themselves with the icy crystals.

The plumage is said to resemble the weather on a bleak wintry day: gray skies above a blanket of snow. On some individuals, probably mature males, the upper coloration is sooty black. But on other males and on females, the grays may be lighter and tinged with brown. Young birds up to their third year retain hints of brown, usually across the shoulders. On first-year birds the browns occasionally blush to pinkish on the sides. There is a wide range of mixed browns and grays to confuse the observer regarding the age and sex of snowbirds in a flock.

Although the majority of *Junco hyemalis* journey far to the north to nest, a trip to the high Appalachians in late spring will afford a chance to hear the liquid, musical territorial song. Juncos return to visit us only in the dead of winter.

The snowbird is exclusively a ground feeder. It descends onto the snowy fields to gather the wasted seeds of weeds and grasses. Swarms of juncos rummage beneath our seed feeders, the dominant individuals flicking their white outer tail feathers as they claim the best pickings. The junco favors millet and cracked small grain over sunflower seed.

CHIPPING SPARROW
Spizella passerina

FIELD MARKS: A uniform red crown covers the head above a white stripe running from the bill to the nape. A thin, black stripe runs through the eye. The bill is dark in the mating season, lighter in winter. The rump is gray, the back is brown, and the tail is notched. The underparts are whitish in nuptial plumage, smoky in winter. The sexes are indistinguishable.
LENGTH: 4¾ inches.
VOICE: The song is a series of rapid chips. Winter notes are single, high-pitched chips.
RANGE IN OUR REGION: Nests throughout. Abandons the northern half of the region in winter, passing the cooler months in southeastern Virginia and in areas east of the mountains in the Carolinas. Further south, it winters west to the Mississippi.
HABITAT: Hedgerows and weedy fields.

The chipping sparrow is one of the tamest of our winter birds. It is one of those species that has benefited from human civilization. The "chippy" has moved readily into the new open spaces created by farming and residential expansion. It nests and winters in the hedgerows, pastures, weedy places and even in the lawns and buildings that man has brought into its range. Indeed, as L. A. Hausman observed regarding the bird's closeness to man, "The song is a familiar dooryard ditty, a sweet, simple reiteration of chip–chip–chip . . . ."

In earlier times when many more homes had their own gardens, orchards, grapevines and livestock, the chipping sparrow was very much a "dooryard" species. With the coming of suburbia and manicured, monoculture lawns, the chippy has been replaced in many residential areas by the aggressive and alien English sparrow. "Hairbird" and "hair sparrow" are among its folk names because it lined its nest with dark horsehair when that was available. Today synthetic fibers find their way into the chipping sparrow's soft nesting cups.

The chipping sparrow can be confused with the swamp sparrow and with the more northerly tree sparrow where their ranges overlap. All have a rusty cap, a light stripe above the eye, and a dark stripe through it. The chipping sparrow is the smallest and has the lightest underparts of the three. It is also the friendliest.

FIELD SPARROW
Spizella pusilla

FIELD MARKS: The sides of the head are gray, the cap a pale rust. There is no streaking on the underparts. The bird has a pink bill and legs, and the tail is notched. The sexes are indistinguishable.
LENGTH: 5 inches.
VOICE: A thin, high series of TSSPs or TSEEs in winter.
RANGE IN OUR REGION: Winters and nests throughout.
HABITAT: Fencerows, abandoned fields with tall grass and weeds.

The field sparrow is a loner. It does not collect in large feeding flocks on the wintering grounds as do many sparrows, including some of its close relatives in the genus *Spizella.* Nor does the field sparrow easily tolerate direct human contact. Its shy and timid manner makes it only an occasional visitor at the seed feeder and a difficult bird to approach in the field. It favors brushy pastures on abandoned farms and avoids cultivated fields and barnyards. Small insects and weed seeds are the staples of the field sparrow's winter diet.

A tawny crown and stripe beginning at the rear of the eye and angling abruptly downward decorate the pale gray head. This coloration continues down the back, and the gray reappears at the base of the notched tail. Two distinct wing bars are visible.

During the breeding season the field sparrow's song is heard in our region. Arthur A. Allen describes the statement as a "CHE-WEE, CHE-WEE beginning slowly then increasing in tempo to a breathless trill. The clear plaintive notes lend an air of melancholy to the countryside." The winter notes are distinctive, high-pitched lisps often lost in the feeding chatter of more numerous wintering sparrows.

The field sparrow nests near the ground, frequently in a briar thicket of multiflora rose or blackberry. An intrusion can fledge the young after half the normal time in the nest, perhaps as soon as their fifth day. The ability to survive a premature fledging is an adaptation common among low-nesting species whose nests are sometimes molested by ground mammals.

WHITE-THROATED SPARROW
Zonotrichia albicollis

FIELD MARKS: The head markings feature alternating black and white stripes from bill to nape, yellow lores, and, in all plumages, a well-defined white throat patch. Markings on immature birds and some fall adults are similar but subdued. The sexes are indistinguishable.
LENGTH: 5¾ inches.
VOICE: A slurred whistle, OOO-TEE-WHEY-WHEY, the second note much higher than the first.
RANGE IN OUR REGION: Winters in all sections. Occasionally nests in mountains and piedmont.
HABITAT: Fencerows, dense underbrush in overgrown fields, along power lines, and in other unforested areas.

The white-throat stays near the ground, often on it. It is perhaps the most common sparrow in our region in winter. It may be seen in large numbers on any winter walk along the edges of woods, in brushy swaths at power lines, and along fencerows. It forages in the densest undergrowth for the seeds of grasses and weeds and for the berries of poke, honeysuckle and privet. Swishing and squeaking sounds made against the back of the hand often draw the inquisitive white-throat to an exposed perch, affording the observer a handsome profile.

Near our homes we see the white-throated sparrow most often scratching on the ground beneath our seed feeders for food wasted by other birds. Under feeders and in wilder settings, it scratches in harmony with juncos, song sparrows and other ground feeders.

To the north of our region, the white-throat's call is interpreted to say "Ooh poor Sam Peabody, Peabody, Peabody"; hence the folk name "Peabody bird." I am unable to hear these suggestions in the white-throat's voice because the final notes, in our region at least, seem to have only one syllable. The common name "whistlejack" seems more fitting because the call is more of a languid, quavering whistle than a series of brisk syllables.

The evening call of the white-throat contributes strongly to the set of sounds that have come to mean winter to us. No less than the junco's feeding note that sounds like thin ice cracking on a pond, the white-throat's vesper BEET, BEET is part of our perception of a winter eve. We hear it on coming home from work at a cold sundown and on our evening trip to the woodpile. From every shrub and cedar in the neighborhood, the explosive notes ring to mark the roosting perches. When heard at dusk from the back porch or from the center of a lonely field, the white-throats' chorus, chiming from the woods' edges and fencerows all around, can make one glad it is winter.

FOX SPARROW
Passerella iliaca

FIELD MARKS: This is the largest sparrow in our region. It is recognized by the rusty tail and rump, streaked underparts and central breast spot. The sexes are indistinguishable.
LENGTH: 6½ inches.
VOICE: A thin, high, incisive TSST on the wintering grounds.
RANGE IN OUR REGION: Winters throughout.
HABITAT: Edges of woods, fencerows.

The fox sparrow is nearly as large as the towhee and is much like it in feeding habit. The big, rusty sparrow forages in the leaf litter, scratching backward with both feet simultaneously. A feeding flock of fox sparrows create a great disturbance in the fallen leaves, as the birds rake into the woodland mulch for seeds and insects. When frightened, the flock flies into the branches of nearby trees and waits patiently for the danger to pass. Fox sparrows are also seen singly, often on the ground beneath a seed feeder with juncos, white-throats and towhees.

The fox sparrow appears to be much larger than any of our other wintering sparrows and sometimes gives the initial impression of being a thrush or even a thrasher. It is easily mistaken for our only wintering thrush, the hermit, because of the approximately equal size and the rusty upper tail coverts of both. The hermit thrush's back, however, is olive, and the breast is spotted. The fox sparrow's back is gray streaked with brown, and the breast markings are reddish streaks. The conical fringillid bill of the fox sparrow is noticeably different from the longer, thinner bill of the thrush.

There are eighteen races of the fox sparrow covering most of the continent during their migratory cycle. Western varieties tend toward dark chocolate and more uniform color, ours toward rustier hues. The seasonal movements cover many thousands of miles, since the birds winter in our region and in the American Southwest and they nest in subarctic sites. On the nesting territories, the song is rich and clear. The wintering notes we hear are quiet lisps by comparison.

SONG SPARROW
Melospiza melodia

FIELD MARKS: The heavily streaked breast bears a central spot. There is a rusty stripe through the eye, one across the cheek, and another down the "chin." The tail is long and slightly rounded. The upperparts vary with locality from gray to rusty. The sexes are indistinguishable.
LENGTH: 5½ inches.
VOICE: The alarm note is a musical TCHERP. The call is a long, high, trilled note introduced by a triplet.
RANGE IN OUR REGION: Winters throughout. Nests to the north of our region.
HABITAT: Marshes, along streams, brushy open spaces.

The song sparrow can be confused with the fox sparrow, for both have streaked breasts and similar head markings. The song sparrow is significantly smaller, and its tail is proportionately longer and more rounded. On the perch the song sparrow nervously flips its tail, and it "pumps" it in flight, causing a dipping flight path.

Its song is this sparrow's best identifier. It can be heard on the nesting territories and on the wintering grounds, especially toward the end of winter. It is an early-migrating bird, one of the first to follow winter northward in spring. Its cheery call, Thoreau said, "helps to crack the ice in the ponds." He interpreted the territorial refrain as "Maids! Maids! Maids! Hang up your teakettle–ettle–ettle." As the northbound migrants invade the territories of permanent residents, epic battles ensue. The combatants sometimes fight vertically for several feet, rising out of the briars as if drawn on strings.

Habitats near the water attract the song sparrow. The bird often haunts the borders of streams and open marshy places, and it winters in great numbers in coastal habitats. "Swamp finch" and "marsh sparrow" are among its common names.

The seeds of grasses and weeds sustain the song sparrow in winter. It enjoys millet and cracked small grains at the seed feeder.

Farther Afield

great blue heron

Scratching Birds *(Order Galliformes)*

FAMILY MELEAGRIDIDAE

TURKEY
Meleagris gallopavo

FIELD MARKS: A large ground-dwelling bird with long, strong legs and short, rounded wings. The head and neck are festooned with wattles grading in color from red to blue, those of the male being the more colorful. Body contour feathers show green, blue and red iridescence. The female is smaller and less iridescent. The male has a tuft of hairlike feathers at the center of the breast.
LENGTH: 36 to 48 inches.
VOICE: A "gobble" similar to that of the domestic turkey.
RANGE IN OUR REGION: Locally resident in lower mountain elevations, piedmont and coastal plain.
HABITAT: Deciduous woods, wooded swamps.

The turkey is the largest land bird in North America. It is native to this continent and once flourished throughout the deciduous habitats of its range. Today it is common only in localities where restocking, habitat preservation and careful management have enabled the great scratching bird to make a comeback.

Like other Galliformes (the scratching birds), turkeys use their long, powerful legs and feet to scratch for food in the leaf litter. The turkey's diet is principally acorns, insects, roots, tubers, nuts, seeds, grasses and berries. The bird is gregarious but not colonial. In early morning, small flocks of a dozen or less feed together, with one or two sentinels keeping watch. The turkeys scratch and pick thoroughly over a half acre, then move on to another feeding area. Toward evening the flock ravishes another tract or two of the forest floor before retiring to the tallest treetops to roost.

Turkeys are supreme runners. John James Audubon once pursued a flock for hours on horseback without

being able to overtake the birds. Moreover, at no time in the chase were the turkeys obliged to take flight. This preference for a running escape has led some to conclude, very much in error, that the turkey is a weak flier. When necessary, even a thirty-five pound tom can quickly clear the treetops and sail a mile or more, flapping only occasionally.

The turkey has an interesting history richly interwoven with that of our nation. The first explorers found the bird a ready source of food from New England to Florida. Early colonists found that the turkey was relatively tame throughout its extensive natural range. The Aztecs had already domesticated it in Mexico. Turkeys were among the first "riches" returned to Europe from the New World by early adventurers, and by 1540 the never-spartan board of Henry VIII groaned under the weight of turkeys raised in England as domestic fowl.

As a wild species in America, however, the turkey fared poorly because of intensive shooting and the destruction of its habitat. The last sighting of a wild specimen in Connecticut was in 1813; in Massachusetts the last wild sighting was recorded in 1851. The destruction of the chestnut trees deprived the turkey, along with many other species of wildlife, of an important food source. Neglect and persecution continued, and by the early twentieth century this great bird was a rarity except in the wildest southern swamps and Appalachian slopes.

Fortunately for us and for the turkey, we live in more enlightened times today. The bird that Benjamin Franklin nominated to be our national symbol once more struts and calls in our woods, reminding us that nature need not be subdued and devastated for man to flourish on this land.

FAMILY TETRAONIDAE

RUFFED GROUSE
Bonasa umbellus

FIELD MARKS: A camouflage-brown ground bird the size of a bantam chicken. The head is crested. The tail is squared but opens to 120 degrees in flight, showing black bands alternating with the basic reddish or gray body color, depending on locality. During courtship the male displays a ruff of dark feathers at the sides of his neck.
LENGTH: 14 inches.
VOICE: Insignificant. However, during courtship the male makes a drumming sound of increasing tempo by thumping the air with his wings.
RANGE IN OUR REGION: Resident in all sections of the Appalachians and Smokies.
HABITAT: Open clearings in deciduous woods. Prefers coniferous tracts in winter.

Atop Mt. Mitchell in North Carolina, the highest mountain east of the Mississippi, a stunted tangle of Frazier fir battles the freezing winter winds for possession of the summit. When I visited this outpost between blizzards in the winter of 1973, I found only two species of birdlife—a large number of dark-eyed juncos and a single ruffed grouse hen. Winter calls the "wood hen," as mountain people know the ruffed grouse, to the coniferous stands to seek shelter in the evergreen boughs and to feed on the buds of shrubs and low trees. The grouse strides confidently across the snow on the feathered projections that grow on its feet in winter. When approached, the grouse waits until its cover is kicked or shaken, then flushes by half skipping, half flying through the brush to emerge on thundering wings, often choosing an escape route that places a large tree between bird and hunter.

The ruffed grouse's immense range spans the northern half of the continent from Alaska to the southern Appalachians. Red and gray color phases occur in coastal and inland regions, respectively. At times the phases can be found in the same locality, even in the same brood.

In late winter the male thumps out his territorial statement by pounding the air with a drum roll of wingbeats quickening its tempo, BUP, BUP, BUP-BUP-UP-URRRRRR. The crest bristles, the tail fans over the cock's back, and the strutting bird displays the glossy black ruff at the sides of his neck. The scholarly ornithologist and prolific writer of bird lore, Arthur Cleveland Bent, called the ruffed grouse's drumming "the throbbing heart of awakening spring." Pennsylvanians, blessed with healthy populations of the handsome game bird, named this cock of the deep woods their state bird.

FAMILY PHASIANIDAE

BOBWHITE
Colinus virginianus

FIELD MARKS: The upperparts have generally a camouflaged brownish pattern. The underparts are barred with rust and white. The head is slightly crested. The male has a white eye stripe and a white patch on the throat; on the female these marks are buff.
LENGTH: 8 inches.
VOICE: A whistled BOB-BOB-WHITE with accent on the surname. The gathering call is a two-note, upward-percolating whistle.
RANGE IN OUR REGION: Resident in all sections.
HABITAT: Open fields, briar thickets, the edges of woods. Avoids deep woods.

♂

The bobwhite is the most sought-after game bird in America, especially in our region. Though some fifteen million are shot annually, the bobwhite's populations are larger and healthier than ever. The bird proliferated as land was cleared during the early settlement of the eastern United States, and more recent management practices, such as the purposeful planting of food and cover, have given the bobwhite an additional boost.

In early spring the territorial song, BOB-WHITE, rings throughout the bird's extensive range from Michigan to Guatemala. Both sexes incubate the clutch of a dozen or more eggs and help raise the highly precocial young, who can fly within less than two weeks. Several families join in winter to form a covey, roosting by night in a tight, outward-facing circle. By day the covey feeds on seeds, buds, berries and other fruit.

The bobwhite is terrestrial, as would be expected of a gallinaceous bird. It runs swiftly when alarmed, the legs a blur of motion. When pressed, the covey waits motionless, then explodes into the air in unison, flying off in all directions. Within three seconds after being flushed, a bobwhite can reach a speed of sixty feet per second and can be out of shotgun range. The challenge to a marksman is great, but the "bird," as the bobwhite is affectionately known, is appreciated even more widely as a songbird and a symbol of nature.

Herons, Egrets and Bitterns *(Order Ciconiiformes)*

FAMILY ARDEIDAE

GREAT BLUE HERON
Ardea herodias

FIELD MARKS: This very large wading bird stands four feet tall. The back and wings are blue-gray; the neck is slightly lighter, whitish down the throat. The head is white with a black crest of rearward-pointing plumes. The thighs are rusty, and the wrists have black markings. The bill and legs are very long. The sexes are indistinguishable.
LENGTH: 42 to 50 inches.
WINGSPAN: 70 inches.
VOICE: Several hoarse squawks in rapid sequence.
RANGE IN OUR REGION: Winters and nests in all sections except the mountains.
HABITAT: Coastal marshes, rivers, lakes and ponds.

The great blue heron is the largest dark wading bird in our region. In the west and midwest it is sometimes confused with the sandhill crane, which does not occur in our region. It is important to note that the great blue heron is not a crane, as evidenced by the S-curve in which the neck is carried in flight.

Wintering in our region, the great blue heron frequently visits inland lakes and ponds. A solitary hunter, it leaves its six-inch tracks in the mud of streams, creeks and rivers as they flow through a variety of habitats. Called "Poor Jo" for its gaunt appearance, the great blue has adapted well to man's presence and to his alterations to the land. It has capitalized on the proliferation of farm ponds. Still, this solitary, stately figure will rise with deep, labored strokes of its six-foot wings to avoid an approaching human hundreds of yards away. The legs sway astern, rudderlike, and the neck strains forward as the huge bird launches. The

head settles back against the shoulders as the wings go into slow motion suggesting the "climbing cruise" power setting of an airplane. The heron croaks a guttural protest on departing.

If we maintain a respectful distance, the great blue will suffer us to observe his hunting, a study in stealth. Eyeing a fish in the shallows, the gaunt wader slowly swings his beak in line with the victim and stalks with slow, deliberate steps, never rippling the water. By Audubon's account, "slowly does he raise his head from his shoulders, and now, what a sudden start! His formidable bill has transfixed a perch, which he beats to death on the ground. See with what difficulty he gulps it down his capacious throat!" Occasionally the great blue lands in deep water to spear fish from a school near the surface. At other times it can be seen eating insects in a plowed field or pasture.

BLACK-CROWNED NIGHT HERON
Nycticorax nycticorax

FIELD MARKS: The crown and back are greenish black, the underparts white. Two long white plumes hang from the rear of the head. Immature birds are brown with white streaks below, white spots above. The eyes are red in adults, yellow in immature birds. The sexes are indistinguishable.

LENGTH: 22 inches.

WINGSPAN: 44 inches.

VOICE: A short, low KWAWK.

RANGE IN OUR REGION: Most abundant in coastal marshes but also winters inland throughout the coastal plain and piedmont.

HABITAT: Inland streams, lakes and ponds. Marshes and estuaries near the coast.

The dark cap and back contrasting with whitish underparts are diagnostic markings. The necks of night herons are shorter and thicker than those of other herons. The black-crowned is the only night heron to winter in our region. Another species, the yellow-crowned, joins the black-crowned in coastal and inland rookeries during the nesting season. Young of both species retain their brown plumage through the first winter and are easily mistaken for the American bittern.

Night herons are nocturnal birds whose short, single notes are heard occasionally in the night sky as the herons travel between ponds or streams. Nocturnal feeding gives this bird ample access to frogs and crayfish, which it hunts by stalking. When fishing, it stands stone still, then strikes explosively when a fish swims into range. Sightings of the species are uncommon because, by day, black-crowned night herons gather in communal roosts ensconced in secluded groves.

The black-crowned occupies a very large range outside North America, including much of Europe and Asia. In Japan it was honored in feudal times by being elevated to a court peerage, and it is still called the *goi* heron, *go-i* signifying the fifth court rank.

AMERICAN BITTERN
Botaurus lentiginosus

FIELD MARKS: Brown patterns camouflage the bittern above and below. The black whisker patch is a good field mark. The dark flight feathers are diagnostic when the bird is flying. The sexes are indistinguishable.
LENGTH: 23 to 34 inches.
WINGSPAN: 45 inches.
VOICE: A pumping UMP-GA-LUMP.
RANGE IN OUR REGION: Winters in coastal zones and inland in all sections except the mountains. Nests in the northern part of our region and northward.
HABITAT: Swamps, freshwater marshes, ponds.

The American bittern is best known for its "freeze," a motionless posture it assumes to avoid detection. The neck extends vertically, and the bill aims skyward while the bittern peers horizontally past its chin. Seen head on, the bittern's head is V-shaped, a configuration that permits the bird to see around its bill when in this defensive posture.

When the bittern "freezes" in the cattails and marsh grass, the vertical patterns on the throat and breast blend effectively with the surroundings. If the wind rustles the reeds, the bittern consummates the camouflage by swaying with the vegetation. This defense is so reliable that the bittern employs it even when in an exposed location, such as a mowed roadside, and will sometimes permit very close approach before abandoning the then-ludicrous ruse.

The American bittern's voice invites picturesque description. Alexander Sprunt, Jr., writes, "Amid violent contortions that make him look as if he were about to retch, the bird gulps air, distending his crop and throat. Then he belches forth a guttural croak like the sound of an old wooden pump: OONG-KA-CHOONK, OONG-KA-CHOONK, OONG-KA-CHOONK." Thoreau observed, "The bittern pumps in the fen." The folk name, "stake driver," derives from the resemblance of the bittern's "song" to the sound of a distant mallet hitting a stake.

Freshwater marshes with tall vegetation are the American bittern's chosen habitat. The marshy edges and backwaters of ponds and large lakes attract the elusive bird. It may be found in such inland locations within its range in any season. The secretive, solitary disposition and the protective coloration make a winter sighting noteworthy.

Most active at dusk and at night, the "thunder pumper" slowly threads through the reeds in search of frogs, fish, crawfish, mice and insects.

Shorebirds, Gulls and Alcids
(Order Charadriiformes)

FAMILY CHARADRIIDAE

KILLDEER
Charadrius vociferus

FIELD MARKS: Two black neck bands and a rusty rump distinguish the killdeer from all other plovers. The underparts, forehead and eye stripe are white; the back and wings are grayish brown. White is visible in the wings and tail in flight. The sexes are indistinguishable.
LENGTH: 8 inches.
VOICE: A strident KILLDEE, KILLDEE, KILLDEE often given in flight; a staccato BEEET-EET-EET-EET upon taking off; a rolling trill on landing.
RANGE IN OUR REGION: Winters in all sections except the mountains. Nests in all sections.
HABITAT: Fields, pastures, edges of ponds; usually inland and often far from water.

The killdeer is the only plover residing inland in our region. Closely cropped pastures with low, moist places are its favored habitat, but this upland member of a seashore clan can be found on dry slopes far from water.

The presence of the killdeer is often revealed by its loud, distinctive and frequently repeated KILLDEE call. It permits humans to approach to within a hundred feet or so, then launches itself with a shrieking staccato protest timed with the beats of its long, thin, pointed wings. The rusty cinnamon patch on the rump and white stripes on the wings mark the killdeer's departure. After circling for some minutes on deep, graceful wing strokes to the tune of its plaintive cries, the killdeer spills its lift in a series of steep banks and glides to earth. The dainty plover hits the ground running, decelerates, then, in a distinctive gesture which displays all its markings, slowly raises its wings and folds them into place. Once on the ground, it runs with swift, fluid sprints on "twinkling" legs, pausing to bob its head up and to utter a tentative trill.

Killdeer feed in plowed fields and closely cropped pastures, avoiding tall grass. They subsidize the farmer by eating ticks, flies and mosquitoes from around livestock and by plucking grasshoppers, beetles and weevils from cultivated plants. I have watched killdeer feeding with snipe in moist spots in pastures, where they pick worms from the surface and probe the mud for grubs and crustaceans.

Vociferus has struck a happy balance with man, though it has not always been so. "Sportsmen" silenced the evocative cries of our dryland plover over much of its range near the turn of the century at about the same time that they were extirpating a host of other species of wildlife. The Carolina parakeet and the passenger pigeon were blasted from our region and never returned; the snowy egret and the killdeer miraculously recovered. Today the killdeer's chorus rings again across our farmlands. In spring the crier nests on gravel rooftops and driveways, limping away with a heart-rending distraction display each time a human approaches the nest.

WOODCOCK
Philohela minor

FIELD MARKS: This is a chunky bird with a long, straight bill, short neck and legs, and a very short tail. The dark eyes are set near the top of the head. The upperparts are intricately patterned in rich browns, grays and black. The underparts are of plain cinnamon color. The sexes are indistinguishable.
LENGTH: 8¼ inches.
VOICE: A loud, nasal PEENT. Warbling chirps are given during the display flight.
RANGE IN OUR REGION: Winters in lower piedmont and coastal plain from New Jersey to the Gulf Coast. Nests in all sections of our region.
HABITAT: Moist woodlands, alder thickets.

If you spend enough time walking along the woodland streams of our region, you are bound to have the experience of flushing a woodcock from beneath your feet. The rotund bird explodes into the air on wings that whistle at each beat as he streaks away through the woods. Mark his landing spot if you will, but he is so effectively camouflaged that you are unlikely to find him unless he flies again.

The woodcock pursues earthworms, its dietary staple, by probing the moist soils with its long prehensile bill. In the soft alluvial mud the sensitive mandibles can feel and grasp an earthworm not visible to the woodcock. While it is feeding, the bird is most concerned visually with what is going on above and behind it. The eyes are set toward the upper rear of the head, giving the woodcock a greater span of binocular vision to the rear than to the front. This reduces the chance that it will be surprised by a predator while feeding.

Because earthworms are most active at night, the woodcock is principally crepuscular and nocturnal. Its nights are spent in search of food; its days, crouching in an alder thicket in avoidance of danger. So we see the "mud snipe" only in a chance encounter, but we know of its presence more often by reading the clusters of deep, small-diameter holes left in the stream-side mud by the woodcock's incessant nighttime probings.

One icy February dusk when I was a young boy, I heard a distant, raspy PEENT which I attributed to a nighthawk. I was confused that the nighthawk, whom I had seen catching insects on soft summer nights, should be in Virginia in midwinter. Every few seconds the single nasal note wafted across the fields to me. I expected the source of the sounds to move, but the call changed only by growing louder as I cautiously approached. I crept to the edge of a clearing from which the calls seemed to be coming, and suddenly a bird burst into flight a few feet away. The wings whistled and, as the chunky bird flew against the dimly lit western sky, I could see that it was a woodcock and knew that I was witnessing the nuptial flight about which I had often read. Upward arced the woodcock to swoop and wheel high above me. The faint whistles of the wings grew more intense, and then I heard the chirping, warbled mating song; it seemed to come down to me from heaven in general rather than from the tiny dot in the darkening sky. At length, the notes stopped abruptly, and the woodcock careened earthward in a headlong, zigzagging dive. Five seconds later the plump little game bird with the comical shape was back on the ground peenting into the darkness. That moving encounter left one of the most delicious memories of my youth. I make it a point now to spend a few prevernal evenings every year attending the woodcock's wedding celebrations.

Joel Arrington

COMMON SNIPE
Capella gallinago

FIELD MARKS: The bill is very long; the legs and tail are longer than those of the woodcock. The upperparts are streaked with dark brown, as is the breast. A white belly, greenish legs and bill, and orange upper tail complete the coloring. The sexes are indistinguishable.
LENGTH: 9 inches.
VOICE: A hoarse, rasping KRZZZT when flushed.
RANGE IN OUR REGION: The wintering range covers the southern half of the United States. In our region the snipe winters inland as far north as Southside Virginia, and much further north along the coast.
HABITAT: Open bogs and marshes; low, wet meadows.

The snipe inhabits moist places in meadows and near ponds. The bird always takes us by surprise, flushing with a single rasping note when we are thirty paces away. Its escape flight follows a low zigzagging course broken by quick, evasive turns.

Experience showed me that I would not be able to photograph the snipe by approaching its boggy habitat and stalking a cooperative individual. I had tried watching the birds from a distance before I attempted to approach. Always, as I drew near, the snipe, clearly visible through binoculars as they fed at leisure, vanished in the scant cover to take flight in quick sequence before I could locate them at a photographable range. Finally I built a blind near a likely spot and spent many delightful hours photographing and watching the snipe along with other birds who frequent grassy, wet meadows.

The snipe usually arrive at their feeding grounds singly and flutter to a landing after diving from a high, swift flight on swept-back, pointed wings. They feed in small groups, probing with rapid stabbing thrusts into the mud for worms and scurrying through the bog in a series of short, abrupt sprints. Killdeer and grackles join the snipe. When danger flushes the other birds, the snipe freeze against clumps of grass, sometimes for as long as a half hour. They are masters of immobility when the occasion demands.

Like the woodcock, the "jacksnipe" performs an elaborate nuptial flight, though we would not expect to see it in our region since the nesting grounds are in Canada, Alaska and the western United States. Unlike the woodcock, the snipe does not vocalize during this flight but spreads its outer tail feathers to make eerie pulsating notes which, by one description, "sound like the sigh of a lost soul."

Pigeons and Doves *(Order Columbiformes)*

Family Columbidae

ROCK DOVE
(Domestic or Street Pigeon)
Columba livia

FIELD MARKS: Variable colors, mostly white, grays and rusts, bedeck this semidomestic alien. The rump is white. Except on all-white individuals, there is a black terminal band on the tail. Iridescence is visible on the neck. The sexes are indistinguishable.
LENGTH: 13 inches.
VOICE: A muttered, bubbling COO-OO-OOO.
RANGE IN OUR REGION: Winters and nests throughout.
HABITAT: Farms, cities.

The slapping of wing tips on takeoff and the high dihedral during glides are characteristics of the flight of the domestic pigeon. Although coloration is variable, the predominant hues are bluish gray.

The domestic pigeon has occupied our barns, urban buildings and statuary since its introduction into North America in colonial times. Its diet is gleaned from streets, fields and refuse piles. The pigeon breeds prolifically in cities, less so on farms, but nowhere do its numbers assume the runaway proportions of the English sparrow's or the starling's, other aliens in North America which, like the pigeon, are semiparasitic on man. Most important, the pigeon does not threaten the ecological niches of any wild native birds.

Domesticated for over five thousand years, the street pigeon is a descendant of the European rock dove, whose natural nesting quarters are caves and ledges on cliffs. Man's genetic tampering has produced varying shapes and colors, but a few generations of natural selection restore the appearance of the original rock dove, approximated by the bird in the photograph.

♀

MOURNING DOVE
Zenaida macroura
(Formerly *Zenaidura macroura*)

FIELD MARKS: Grayish brown plumage with a few dark spots covers the back; the breast is lighter with tinges of pink. The slender, pointed tail is half the bird's length. The male wears a powder blue crown and beads of iridescence along the sides of the neck.
LENGTH: 11 inches.
VOICE: Low, mournfully gentle cooings, COO-AH, COO, COO, COO, given mostly in spring.
RANGE IN OUR REGION: Winters and nests in all sections.
HABITAT: Suburbs, farmlands, harvested grain fields.

The mourning dove is the only wild dove common in our region. The startling whiffle of wings when this dove takes flight is a diagnostic sound. Only the woodcock's wings make a comparable, but not similar, whistling noise. The mourning dove is principally a ground feeder, gleaning wasted grain and weed seeds from the fields. It is a frequent visitor to pastures and barnyards, and to the ground beneath bird feeders.

Though it winters throughout most of its breeding range, the mourning dove is a migratory species, and the individuals wintering in our region may nest farther north. A pair of doves begins nesting in February and continues through October, raising over this long nesting span as many as five broods of two young each. The doves feed their hatchlings first a curdy secretion from the lining of the parent birds' crops and, later, regurgitated seeds. The familiar, doleful COO-AH, COO, COO, COO rings across the fields on the first warm days of late winter and continues through the nesting season. The call is sometimes misidentified as that of an owl.

In most northern states the mourning dove is protected as a songbird. Throughout the South the shooting of doves is a popular group sport, though not without its critics. My own observation is that less than half the doves shot are recovered; many fall into cover or are merely wounded by inept marksmen. There are few scenes more pathetic than a popular "dove field" on Sunday morning after Labor Day weekend's opening day, with the wounded doves limping and flopping in search of food and water.

The "split season" has a particularly gruesome effect on doves. Several states, North Carolina being one, split the dove season into two parts, the first in early September and the second after Thanksgiving. Doves are still nesting during the first hunting season, so the young whose parents are shot die on the nest. Moreover, a high proportion of nesting females is killed because, during the day, the males are home incubating while the females feed. The females typically incubate at night. Authorities argue that the doves migrate early and will be lost if not "harvested" in the September season. There is also the contention that populations of doves are healthy and can withstand the shooting pressure. To many this is an unconscionable violation of the principle of wildlife management that game should not be molested during the breeding season. To others the shooting of the international symbol of peace is barbaric under any circumstances.

Kingfishers *(Order Coraciiformes)*

FAMILY ALCEDINIDAE

BELTED KINGFISHER
Megaceryle alcyon

FIELD MARKS: The kingfisher's silhouette is distinguished by a large head with ragged crest and long, pointed bill and by a small body. The head and upper surfaces are blue. A white collar separates the blue of the breast band from that on the head. A white spot lies between the eye and the base of the bill. Only the female wears a rusty band across the breast.
LENGTH: 12 inches.
VOICE: A raucous rattle suggesting a New Year's Eve noisemaker.
RANGE IN OUR REGION: Winters and nests throughout the Carolinas and nearby states; abandons higher elevations in northern Virginia, Maryland and southern Pennsylvania in winter.
HABITAT: Near running streams, lakes, marshes, tidal creeks and waters of the coastal sounds.

One of the rewards of walking along a woodland stream is to hear the rattling call of an approaching kingfisher as it scuds beneath the arched alders. We can not but pause and watch as the blue missile flashes past along the watercourse on powerful but irregular wingbeats, noisily proclaiming its fishing territory.

The belted is the only kingfisher in our region. It is seen singly, but commonly, in favorable habitats which offer clean water and handy hunting perches. The kingfisher prefers to hunt along streams for daces, shiners, chubs, sculpins and other small fish typically grouped under the colloquial heading of "minnows." The prey

♀

is usually those fish that are destructive to the fry of trout and other fish prized by anglers.

The kingfisher hunts by perching motionless on a wire or exposed snag, sometimes for long periods, searching the water's surface for the ripple of a small fin. Spotting its quarry, the fisherman dives headlong into the water, catching the fish in its long, pointed beak. It erupts from the water, returns to the perch, and cracks the fish's head against the snag before swallowing it headfirst. Sometimes the kingfisher sweeps low over the water, then climbs to hover above prospective prey. Except for the terns, the belted kingfisher is the only small bird in our region that dives headfirst into the water from hovering flight.

At mating time a pair of kingfishers share the work of digging a tunnel three to fifteen feet into a wall of sand or clay, often in a stream bank or road cut. In a domed chamber deep in the tunnel the female warms the eggs. Because her nesting duties do not expose her as an easy target for predation, the female belted kingfisher has no need of protective coloration. Accordingly, she sports a rusty band across her chest where the male has none. This decoration makes her one of the world's few female birds with plumage more colorful than that of her mate.

Woodpeckers *(Order Piciformes)*

FAMILY PICIDAE

RED-HEADED WOODPECKER
Melanerpes erythrocephalus

FIELD MARKS: Strongly contrasting blocks of black and white show in flight. The entire head from the shoulders upward is blood red. At rest, the clean white on the underparts and on the secondary flight feathers is set against the glossy black back and shoulders, suggesting formal attire. The sexes are indistinguishable.
LENGTH: 7½ inches.
VOICE: A polyglot of calls including a loud KWEE-OH resembling the call of the crested flycatcher. And, as an old field guide describes the vocalizations, "something like the *wicker* of the flicker but gobbled and garbled on its way out; and sundry cacklings, chatterings, chirpings, and squawkings, all more or less raucous."
RANGE IN OUR REGION: Winters and nests throughout. Migrates irregularly depending on food supply.
HABITAT: Open mature deciduous woods. Often seen on older trees in towns.

The red-headed is our most colorful woodpecker. The scarlet head above black and white body parts is diagnostic. More white shows in flight than at rest, the trailing edges of the wings and the upper rump presenting a snowy mark by which the eye can follow the swift, undulating flight. The male of every other woodpecker in the eastern United States has red somewhere on the head, but only the red-headed has an *entirely* red head. Several woodpeckers, especially the red-bellied, are mistaken for the red-headed, but once seen, the red-headed is unforgettable. Through their first winter, the young retain an ash brown plumage with mottled white on the lower back. The plumage of the male and female adults is identical, but the plumage of the young is so markedly different from that of the adults that colonists believed them distinct species.

Audubon described the red-headed's demeanor as "gay, frolicsome." The modern observer, seeing the bird adapt to urban life in established neighborhoods shaded by mature hardwoods, might describe the behavior as calm and urbane. A capable carpenter, the red-headed is partial to creosote-treated utility poles. It sometimes riddles the hardened poles with nesting and roosting cavities as well as numerous lesser sculptures, seemingly made in contempt of human technology rather than in search of insects.

The diet includes a wide variety of plant and animal material. Beetles and their larvae, drilled from decaying wood, comprise the main insect portion. The red-headed can also be seen catching insects on the wing. I watched one leave an idle perch in a maple and, with an audible snap, catch a lacewing in flight 150 feet away over the parking lot of the Carolina Inn in Chapel Hill. It returned to the same perch, stuffed the insect into a crack, and began to preen. A single adult has been known to feed over six hundred insects to its young in an hour.

The vegetable portion of the red-headed's diet features fruits and nuts. In the early 1800's an observer described the red-headed woodpecker's fondness for cherries with this grim calculation: "I may safely assert that a hundred have been shot upon a single cherry tree in one day." That observer was John James Audubon. If the principal bird lover of the time could watch or participate in such a persecution, we must be thankful that any of our wildlife survived the era.

There is a predatory side to the red-headed's personality. Audubon accused it of sucking the eggs of small birds and killing the young. An 1893 report from Ohio described a single red-headed wiping out a colony of cliff swallows nesting on a barn. The woodpecker broke the clay nests and ate the eggs and young. More recently, one was seen attacking a mouse in a city street. Perhaps we can hope that in the parts of our towns where old shade trees afford this handsome bird its necessary habitat, it might turn its predatory attentions toward the alien starlings and English sparrows as well as the mice.

YELLOW-BELLIED SAPSUCKER
Sphyrapicus varius

FIELD MARKS: Both sexes have red caps. The male's chin and bib are red, the female's white. Black and white alternate in the facial markings. The back is mottled white on black; the light underparts are tinged with yellow.
LENGTH: 7¾ inches.
VOICE: A mewing cry.
RANGE IN OUR REGION: Winters throughout the Carolinas and neighboring states; nests in high Appalachians and regions to the north.
HABITAT: Deciduous woods, orchards, wooded urban and suburban neighborhoods.

This medium-sized woodpecker feeds by drilling a series of small holes through the bark and cambium of living wood and eating the sap which seeps into these wells. It balances its diet with insects attracted to the sap, picking them casually from the surfaces of trees but not chiseling into deadwood to get them, as do other woodpeckers. Many species of birds drink from the sapsucker's wells, and in summer hummingbirds and sapsuckers sometimes dine together. White oak, sweet gum and red maple are among the trees that the sapsucker taps, but pecan and fruit trees are especially favored.

Controversy surrounds the effects of sapsuckers' drillings on trees. Disease sometimes results, but the overall effect is minimal because the wounds heal quickly and only a few wells are kept active simultaneously on a given tree. It is not unusual to see robustly healthy fruit trees ringed with the horizontal patterns diagnostic of the sapsucker's enterprises. It is disappointing that science has not yet discovered any benefits the trees derive from the bird's seemingly abusive feeding habits. Such a one-sided relationship contrasts strongly with that maintained by our other wintering woodpeckers, who zealously de-bug the trees and pulverize the dead wood for quicker recycling of its borrowed energy and nutrients.

Because of its unique and specialized feeding preferences, the yellow-bellied sapsucker is usually indifferent to human offerings. Individuals sometimes develop a taste for beef suet, but most are content with the gustatory joys of tree sap.

The sapsucker flies in undulating swoops, proceeding through the woods as if by trapeze. Alighting on the upswing, it works at one set of wells for an extended period, then moves, perhaps, to the sunny side of the tree trunk to rest and preen. The sapsucker will permit close approach, relying on its bark-matching, mottled, white-on-black markings to avoid detection. Our least noisy woodpecker, the yellow-belly occasionally breaks silence with an almost comic catlike cry. Of course, being a woodpecker, it communicates also by drumming a characteristic series on a resonant dead limb—a short burst of diminishing tempo followed by two single taps.

Perching Birds *(Order Passeriformes)*

EASTERN PHOEBE
Sayornis phoebe

FIELD MARKS: The upperparts are uniform grayish brown to smoky black, the underparts are whitish, and the sides are tinged with gray. There are no wing bars, no eye rings or other distinctive features of coloration. The sexes are indistinguishable.
LENGTH: 6 inches.
VOICE: A drawn-out FEEE-BEEE and a one-note CHIP of irritation.
RANGE IN OUR REGION: Winters throughout the North Carolina piedmont and southward. Nests north of the same line into southern Canada. Wintering and nesting ranges overlap in a narrow band across the southeastern United States, from North Carolina to Texas, deepening west of the Mississippi.
HABITAT: Open areas near wooded borders, usually near water.

The eastern phoebe is the only flycatcher wintering in the eastern United States. This relatively tame bird spends the coldest winter days foraging for seeds and berries, but whenever temperatures permit insects to fly, the phoebe stands ready to intercept them. The phoebe waits on an exposed limb or snag for an insect to take wing or for a spider to billow past, then tosses itself into the air and snatches the prey with an audible snap. The junco-colored flycatcher floats lightly back to the hunting perch, swallows, wipes its beak and rictal bristles, and contentedly pumps its tail up and down a few times. The erect posture and the handling of the tail are diagnostic features; the tail normally wags loosely with the breeze except for an occasional vertical twitch.

Food is known to include bugs, beetles, wasps, bees, flies, ticks, spiders and dragonflies. The phoebe relentlessly pursues these insects along the edge of winter, timing its migrations to the availability of its prey. The bird retreats no farther south in winter than is necessary to retain access to its flying food. Still, some errant members of the species winter as far north as New England.

It was Audubon who determined that individual phoebes return to nest at the same spot year after year. His silver thread tied loosely to the phoebes' legs may have been the first banding of birds for scientific purposes. The phoebe's natural nesting sites include rocky crags and irregularities (not cavities) in trees, but the bird has found immediate profit in man-made nesting shelters, such as bridges, porch eaves and unused farm machinery.

HORNED LARK
Eremophila alpestris

FIELD MARKS: The back and wings are cinnamon brown, the underparts whitish. A small bib and a downward-curved mark through the eye are black. A black crown line borders the yellow facial markings and terminates in tiny black "horns" above the eyes. The female's markings are paler.
LENGTH: 7½ inches.
VOICE: On the wintering grounds a faint TINK and high, subdued, buzzing whistles.
RANGE IN OUR REGION: Winters and nests throughout. Most abundant near the coast in winter.
HABITAT: Open fields with short grass, manured fields, coastal sand dunes.

Small flocks of horned larks winter in the short-grassed pastures and bare places of our region, where they scratch for weed seeds and insects. Coastal sands are favored feeding places, as are school playing fields, airports, golf courses and other closely cropped flat-lands with bare patches. The larks run swiftly about their foraging errands and, if prodded, take flight in a compact flock. They return to earth no farther away than prudence requires. Faint tinkling notes and high-pitched, sibilant whistles can be heard coming from the feeding larks.

The horned lark is the only native member of the lark family, a clan of celebrated songsters ranging over Europe, Asia and northern Africa. The horned lark occupies the continent comprehensively, with over twenty races recognized between Alaska and southern Mexico and eastward to Georgia. Though less spectacular than the Old World skylark's aerial opera, the horned lark's nuptial flight song of irregular, jingling notes reminded one observer of the sound of sleigh bells coming from the heavens. The display is accompanied by strutting and posturing on the ground.

The "horns," tiny plumes that project from the sides of the crown, are often difficult to see in the field, as is another distinguishing feature, the elongated hind claw on each foot. The bold black facial pattern and bib are diagnostic. Pale yellow is visible in the faces of mature males and to a lesser extent on females. First-year birds have subdued markings.

FAMILY CORVIDAE

COMMON CROW
Corvus brachyrhynchos

FIELD MARKS: All parts of the crow are glossy black, including the eyes, legs and bill. The tail is rounded in flight. The sexes are indistinguishable.
LENGTH: 17 inches.
VOICE: A series of loud, clear CAW, CAW, CAWs.
RANGE IN OUR REGION: Nests and winters throughout.
HABITAT: Occupies all habitats except the centers of large cities and vast coniferous tracts.

The camera recorded this common crow at the instant it closed the nictitating membrane over its eye.

The steady, labored, rowing wingbeat differentiates the common crow from soaring birds such as the black and turkey vultures. The raucous, clear cawing notes distinguish it from the slightly smaller fish crow. In the redoubts of the common raven high in the Appalachians, the crow's rounded fan of a tail contrasts with the huge raven's V-shaped empennage. In many habitats even a careful observer can momentarily mistake the common crow in flight for a pileated woodpecker or for any of several hawks. The flight characteristic to remember is that the crow never soars, and rarely glides.

Most literature on the common crow includes Henry Ward Beecher's observation that if men wore feathers and wings, very few of them would be clever enough to be crows. The crow's ability to count, to detect firearms, and in general to avoid danger from humans is often the topic of nature lovers' anecdotes. Crows have needed all their wits and resources to survive a long history of intensive persecution by humans.

Where guns and poison have failed, blasting the roosts with dynamite has killed thousands.

In areas where crows were once exterminated, the pests they had controlled multiplied sufficiently to cause much greater economic damage than had the crows. Crows feed heavily on crop-damaging insects such as caterpillars, grasshoppers and beetles. Mice are frequently in the diet. When I once asked an ornithologist what to feed an injured crow I was caring for, he replied, "Give him a mouse and watch what happens." The crow severed the mouse with a few blows of its heavy, all-purpose beak and greedily gulped down the two halves. Vegetation including cultivated grain is also important food for the crow,

FISH CROW
Corvus ossifragus

FIELD MARKS: The bird is entirely black and is similar in every aspect to the common crow, though slightly smaller. The bill is also slightly smaller in proportion to the head. The sexes are indistinguishable.
LENGTH: 15 inches.
VOICE: An unenthusiastic, nasal CA-R or CAH. Sometimes a croaked AH-UK.
RANGE IN OUR REGION: Nests and winters in the coastal plain along the Atlantic and Gulf coasts, thinning inland.
HABITAT: Usually found near coastal and tidal waters.

though the bird is equally at home dining on garbage and carrion.

Crows nest in single-family territories, but in the winter they become gregarious. Flocks varying from a few individuals to several thousand forage in winter pastures and grain fields. Still larger multitudes gather in communal roosts, creating a din audible over great distances. The same raucous calling attends the physical and verbal abuse crows heap upon any hawk or owl caught in the flock's territory.

In the photograph above a common crow chases a red-tailed hawk. The crow, in turn, is often harried in flight by the kingbird in our region during summer. Many birds attack larger species, relying on maneuverability for a safety margin. They are motivated by sport, perhaps, and certainly by the need for territorial defense. Stanley Alford, an experienced field naturalist, told me of watching a red-tailed hawk give occasional spastic movements in an otherwise unperturbed flight; field glasses revealed a hummingbird in furious pursuit.

It is impractical to attempt to distinguish the fish crow from the common crow by appearance. Both are entirely black and are similarly shaped. The common crow is slightly larger, but variation among individuals can result in overlapping sizes between the species. Even where the ranges coincide and the two corvids feed in mixed flocks, they can be difficult to separate visually.

The voices, however, are distinct. A traveler from inland who is not familiar with the fish crow may remark, as did Olin Sewall Pettingill, Jr., that crows near the coast "sound as if they are suffering from bad colds." Actually the traveler is hearing, of course, the short, hoarse notes of the fish crow. Along some sound and coastal waters these indifferent gurgles completely replace the common crow's strong, clear caws.

Like the common crow, the fish crow has adapted handsomely to the presence of humans. Fish crows typically scavenge near wharves and in other fruitful parts of coastal cities. They prey upon the eggs and young of pigeons and starlings nesting on urban build-

ings. I have seen them roosting in the trees on the White House lawn in Washington, D.C., circling the dome of the nation's Capitol, and rummaging in the trash in the parking lots of the Pentagon. I note that they forage as casually at the centers of power as along remote tidal creeks.

The fish crow's natural food covers the wide range expected of corvids but concentrates on marine invertebrates and seashore carrion. Fruit, berries, nuts, seeds, insects and crustaceans are important in the diet, while the eggs and young of other birds are a fish crow's delicacy.

BROWN CREEPER
Certhia familiaris

FIELD MARKS: The thin, downward-curved bill and stiff, pointed tail feathers are diagnostic. The slender body is covered in mixed grays and browns above, white below. There is a white stripe above the eye. The sexes are indistinguishable.
LENGTH: 4¾ inches.
VOICE: A single, very high, thin hissing note.
RANGE IN OUR REGION: Winters throughout. Nests in high Appalachians as far south as eastern Tennessee and western North Carolina.
HABITAT: Coniferous and mixed forests.

Gripping with elongated claws and bracing against the bark with its pointed tail feathers, the brown creeper spirals up tree trunks in a series of short, quick scoots. Reaching a height of thirty feet or so, the creeper flies to the base of the next tree to repeat its upward quest for invertebrates dwelling in the bark. Occasionally the observer hears a nearly ultrasonic TSSS which seems to come from no direction in particular and is hard to associate with the bird.

When the shadow of a hawk crosses the forest, the creeper freezes, becoming only a ghostly shading in the tree bark. So perfect is the bird's camouflage that it seems visible only when moving; in the half-second stops between its upward hitches, the creeper momentarily vanishes.

Wintering in our region, the creeper is seen singly, though sometimes in company with nuthatches and pine warblers. With the bole, limbs and needles of a tree being scoured respectively by these three species, one wonders how a single invertebrate could survive

WINTER WREN
Troglodytes troglodytes

FIELD MARKS: The very short tail is held erect. The chocolate brown upperparts and buff underparts are finely barred with very dark brown, though from a few feet away the bird appears to be of uniform color. The eye stripe is barely noticeable. The sexes are indistinguishable.

LENGTH: 3¼ inches.

VOICE: The winter alarm note is KIP, KIP–KIP almost identical to that of the song sparrow. John Burroughs called the fifelike territorial song, which is heard to the north of our region, "a wild sweet rhythmical cadence that holds you entranced."

RANGE IN OUR REGION: Winters in all parts of the Carolinas and nearby states except for the high Appalachians.

HABITAT: Prefers the banks of wooded streams and other wooded wetlands for its wintering habitat.

on its surface. The creeper is inconspicuous in its woodland habitat and is nowhere numerous; one or two might be sighted in an afternoon's outing in the woods. Its attitude toward humanity is one of disregard, and it occasionally lights at the base of a tree near a hiker, affording a close look. An individual creeper infrequently develops a taste for a mixture of cornmeal, bacon fat and peanut butter and presents itself for observation at the feeding station in a yard thickset with trees.

This is the smallest North American wren and one of the most difficult of our wintering birds to meet. The winter wren is exceptionally shy and keeps to the more remote wooded wetlands. Walking along a stream, I usually become aware of this minute bird by its brief irritation notes. Though the wren may be no more than a few feet away, I get only a fleeting glimpse as it flits among the exposed tree roots and vanishes like a rodent beneath the lip of topsoil overhanging the top of the stream bank. Sighting this uncommon bird, however briefly, can be the highlight of a day's outing. Such an encounter is usually achieved only on a strenuous trek into the tangled wooded bottomlands favored by the "mouse wren."

There is no mistaking the winter wren for any other bird wintering in our region. The brown creeper shares the habitat and might be a candidate in size and color, but it easily differentiates itself by creeping up the tree trunks, using its tail as a prop. The winter wren's little nub of a tail is always held erect. It lacks any markings visible beyond a few feet. The much larger and more vocal Carolina wren displays an obvious white stripe above the eye.

Thirty-five subspecies of the winter wren inhabit the northern hemisphere from the Pribilof Islands across North America to Iceland and into northern Europe and Asia. Many of the races are not migratory, though ours is strongly so. It nests in our region only occasionally in the highest peaks of the southern Appalachians and clearly prefers the spruce forests north of the Great Lakes during the domestic season. Consequently we rarely hear the fine, sweet, tinkling, music-box-like territorial song which Thoreau wrote "was so incessant that at length you noticed it only when it ceased." Wherever and whenever seen, this secretive mite will be bobbing up and down as if on springs, scouring the thickets for ants, caterpillars, spiders, beetles and other small invertebrates.

FAMILY MIMIDAE

BROWN THRASHER
Toxostoma rufum

FIELD MARKS: The upperparts are a rich rufous brown; the underparts are not spotted. The tail is as long as the body, the eyes are yellow, and the bill is long and curved. The sexes are indistinguishable.
LENGTH: 10 inches.
VOICE: Like the other Mimidae, the thrasher has a rich, emphatic song. It sings its phrases twice instead of once (as does the catbird) or several times (as does the mockingbird). An old interpretation goes: "Plant-a-seed, plant-a-seed; drop-it, drop-it; cover-it-up, cover-it-up; pull-it, pull-it; eat-it-all, eat-it-all," etc.
RANGE IN OUR REGION: Nests throughout; abandons higher elevations in winter.
HABITAT: Shrubs and fencerows in clearings. Ornamental shrubs in lawns.

This is the only thrasher east of the Rockies and central Texas. Georgia claims the thrasher for its state bird. In the Carolinas it is sometimes mistaken in winter, as it feeds on the ground, for the slightly smaller fox sparrow, and for the wood thrush in summer. The very long tail and yellow eye are diagnostic.

The thrasher is usually found near the ground. The nests are rarely higher than eye level. The bird feeds principally on the ground, "thrashing" vigorously in the leaves. The thrasher picks among the ground litter, tossing leaves in all directions with sideways strokes of its bill. The ground-foraging rufous-sided towhee also feeds in a storm of agitated leaves but causes its disturbance by scratching, rather than tossing the litter with its bill. The thrasher's food in winter is largely insects found lurking in the litter, small acorns,

and the persistent fruits of shrubs. It enjoys taking, beneath the feeder, millet seed and suet scraps tossed to the ground by other birds. It may visit the birdbath even in the dead of winter.

Like the mocker, the thrasher is aggressive. It will charge a feeding flock of juncos and white-throated sparrows, dispersing one and all to claim the pickings for itself. It will attack cats, dogs, snakes and humans to protect its nest. Still we must count the thrasher a shy bird, since it normally leaves its shrub or thicket only when humanity is at a safe distance.

ROBIN
Turdus migratorius

FIELD MARKS: Orange, not red, is the breast color. The upperparts are gray-brown except for the white tips of the outer tail feathers. The male's head is darker than the female's. The throat is white with dark streaks. The young have spotted breasts.
LENGTH: 10 inches.
VOICE: A sharp, descending KWIT, KWIT, KWIT, KWIT when alarmed or irritated. The territorial song, usually given at dusk, is a caroling series of varying three-syllable phrases, CHEERY-UP, CHEERILY, CHEE-YODLE, etc.
RANGE: Winters and nests throughout.
HABITAT: Moist lawns and pastures, damp woods.

The migratory ways of the robin are not apparent to residents of the Carolinas and nearby states because the bird is with us in all seasons. The individuals who winter with us, however, move northward to nest as the vast populations of robins shift seasonally within their range. Those who nest with us may have wintered along the Gulf Coast or as far south as Guatemala. In regions to the north of ours, which the robin quits in the coldest months, the northward return of the continent's largest thrush breaks winter's grip on the human spirit.

Wintering in our lawns, pastures and woodlands, robins thrust into the sod for earthworms and beetle larvae. On warm winter days a robin may recline on a southward-facing slope, its wings outstretched on the ground, to bask in the sun. One February day I was able to approach to within a few feet of several robins who seemed oblivious to their surroundings as they stared worshipfully at the late afternoon sun.

♂

On winter evenings robins gather in communal roosts in moist woodlands. Large gatherings are more difficult to find now than they were a few decades ago, though the robin population shows no evidence of decline. In 1935, a newspaper account told of hundreds of thousands of robins roosting near Chapel Hill, North Carolina, in a swamp, breaking down trees with the weight of their bodies, and raising a tumultuous din. In Audubon's time, these gatherings occasioned a "sort of jubilee," in his words, at which the great ornithologist observed: "Every gunner brings them home by bagsful, and the markets are supplied with them at a very cheap rate. Several persons may at this season stand round the foot of a tree loaded with berries, and shoot the greater part of the day, so fast do the flocks of Robins succeed each other. They are then fat and juicy, and can afford excellent eating."

The robin is now protected by law from shooting but is subjected to wholesale poisoning by agricultural and garden pesticides. The street which passes my home in Carrboro, North Carolina, is frequently smudged with the flattened remains of robins who had been too sluggish from ingested poisons to get out of the path of an automobile. The robins, of course, are a vastly more effective and economical means of insect control, but they can't afford quite as many prime-time TV commercials to promote themselves as can the chemical conglomerates.

For evolution enthusiasts, the robin offers an example of the early genetic adage "ontogeny recapitulates phylogeny," meaning that the development of an individual reenacts the evolutionary history of its species. Young robins wear spots on their breasts, which many other members of the family Turdidae retain in adulthood.

HERMIT THRUSH
Catharus guttatus
(Formerly *Hylocichla guttata*)

FIELD MARKS: A rusty rump and tail contrast with an olive-brown back. The upper breast and flanks are marked with spotty streaks on a milky background. At rest the bird raises its tail, then lets it drop slowly. The sexes are indistinguishable.

LENGTH: 6 inches.

VOICE: On the wintering grounds, a simple QUOIT or CHUK when disturbed. The territorial song on the northern nesting grounds is elaborate, melodic.

RANGE IN OUR REGION: Winters in all sections except the higher mountain elevations. Does not nest in our region.

HABITAT: Deciduous wooded slopes and swamps.

Wintering deep in the deciduous woods of our region, the hermit thrush is truly a recluse. The bird is seen singly and away from civilization. Upon being approached by a human, it interrupts its feeding in the fallen leaves to fly to a low perch thirty or so yards away. There the hermit slowly raises and lowers its tail in "annoyance" and protests the intrusion into its wooded inner sanctum with an occasional low monosyllable. The rusty rump and tail and olive-brown back is a reverse of the color scheme of the wood thrush, a summer bird in our region, and the bill is slightly shorter. The hermit is the only thrush to winter in the United States.

On the nesting grounds in Canada, Alaska and the Rockies, the hermit is most expressive. The territorial song is an elaborate composition that sounds like flutes and silver bells. Some hail the hermit on its nesting territory as the most evocative North American singer and compare it to the nightingale of Europe.

Unfortunately the hermit shows us only the silent side of its personality while picking in the leaf litter of our region in winter. It avoids areas of continual freezing temperatures and snow cover, which hides the litter-dwelling staples of its diet—snails, spiders, slugs, insects and other small invertebrates. The hermit garnishes these morsels with occasional supplements of fruit and berries.

GOLDEN-CROWNED KINGLET
Regulus satrapa

FIELD MARKS: A very small bird with clearly visible black and white stripes above the eyes. The upperparts are olive greenish; the underparts are lighter, grading to white under the chin and belly. The female's crown is lemon yellow; the male's is orange-yellow with a crimson central crest which can be erected or concealed.

LENGTH: 3½ inches.

VOICE: A thin, high TSEE, TSEE on the wintering grounds. A stronger, more elaborate series on the nesting territory.

RANGE IN OUR REGION: Winters throughout. Nests in high Appalachians as far south as Tennessee and North Carolina.

HABITAT: Prefers conifers but also visits hardwoods.

Stanley Alford

The golden-crowned kinglet is a colorful version of the ruby-crowned. Both sexes of the golden-crowned display the yellow marking on the top of the head at all times. The male reddens the center of his crown by erecting a fiery crest when annoyed. A black stripe and a white stripe show prominently between the eye and the crown. Two white bars decorate the wings. The silhouette is very similar to that of the ruby-crowned, but the golden-crowned's coloration clearly distinguishes the two.

The golden-crowned winters in virtually all parts of our region. It is slightly more tolerant of cold than the ruby-crowned, who shares all but the northern edge of the golden-crowned's wintering range. In our region, the two kinglets are often seen together in mixed flocks. Both are partial to conifers, which they scrutinize crevice by crevice on the bark and cones for insects and other small invertebrates. The golden-crowned tends to feed at a higher level in the trees than does its congener.

Several life histories I have read state that the golden-crowned kinglet is a notably tame bird, sometimes coming close enough for humans to touch. I suspect this may be more true on the nesting territories to the north than on the wintering grounds. (Many birds of the far north show little fear of man.) In our region the bird is aloof and unresponsive to human gestures, including offerings of food. If you "swish" or "squeak" at a mixed party of kinglets, it is most likely that the ruby-crowneds will come down to investigate while the golden-crowneds stick to their business in the upper branches.

FAMILY MOTACILLIDAE

WATER PIPIT
Anthus spinoletta

FIELD MARKS: The upperparts are an unstreaked grayish brown; the underparts are lightly streaked. White outer tail feathers show in flight. The bill and toes are long and slender. The sexes are indistinguishable.

LENGTH: 5½ inches.

VOICE: The PIPIT call is often given in flight.

RANGE IN OUR REGION: Winters in the lower piedmont and in the coastal plain as far north as Maryland. The wintering territory skirts the southern end of the Appalachians.

HABITAT: Plowed fields, meadows, barren rocky areas and other open spaces—most abundant along coasts.

Scattered companies of water pipits winter with us in the open fields of the piedmont and the coastal plain. Feeding on the ground on seeds and insects and along the water's edge on small mollusks and crustaceans, the pipits daintily walk or run (instead of hopping) and pause occasionally to look around and bob their heads. When approached too closely, pipits rise and wheel gracefully on long pointed wings to settle elsewhere in the field and resume feeding. A characteristic flight pattern is the "stair-step" descent profile.

Though water pipits are a common wintering species in the lowlands of our region, we tend to see them only occasionally. They are shy birds who blend well with the grass or with the bare earth of a plowed field. They move swiftly along the ground and usually like to keep fifty yards or more between them and an approaching human. We are more likely to notice them in the air, passing high overhead, repeating their name.

The nesting grounds of the water pipit are far to the north of our region, on the arctic tundra and in the high Rockies. They are reported to nest at altitudes up to five thousand feet on the slopes of Mt. McKinley in Alaska. I have seen them nesting at eleven thousand feet in the Wyoming Rockies, far above the timberline.

FAMILY BOMBYCILLIDAE

CEDAR WAXWING
Bombycilla cedrorum

FIELD MARKS: A black mask and a long, soft crest decorate the head; the tail is tipped with a yellow band. The secondary flight feathers of mature males have horny, flattened tips resembling droplets of red sealing wax.
VOICE: A high, wheezing WHEE-WHEE.
LENGTH: 5¾ inches.
RANGE IN OUR REGION: Winters throughout; nests as far south as North Carolina and Tennessee in the Appalachians and Smokies.
HABITAT: Partially open spaces and woods; often seen in trees and shrubs in urban and residential areas.

Waxwings travel in compact flocks of a dozen or two during the winter, feeding together with harmonious goodwill. They sometimes shuttle in a nearly continuous two-way stream between the tree in which they are feeding and a nearby tree in which they rest between feedings. Favored foods include the fruits of black gum, crab apple, poke, wild grapes and many ornamental shrubs. Holly and pyracantha near human dwellings often bring them in for close observation.

Members of a feeding flock can be seen affectionately passing berries or blossom petals from bird to bird, soothing one another all the while with their sweet, lisping conversation.

Waxwings are relatively tame, especially in urban areas, which are perhaps their favored wintering habitats. They often flee more readily before the cantankerous assaults of the mockingbird than from the approach of an interested human. I have stood directly in the stream of a flock of waxwings shuttling between holly trees with the birds passing within a few feet of my head.

The cedar waxwing nests late, waiting in our region until perhaps June before migrating northward. This schedule permits the fruits to ripen on the northern nesting grounds just as the waxwings arrive.

FAMILY PARULIDAE

PALM WARBLER
Dendroica palmarum

FIELD MARKS: Helpful identifiers include the chestnut cap above a yellow eye stripe and the yellow underparts, especially the undertail coverts. The yellow breast is lightly streaked with rust. The constantly bobbing tail is diagnostic. The sexes are indistinguishable.
LENGTH: 5 inches.
VOICE: A faint, high series of SWITs.
RANGE IN OUR REGION: Winters throughout the lower piedmont and coastal plain of our region and to the south. Nests in Canada.
HABITAT: Seen on or near the ground in brushy fields, fencerows, gardens, lawns. Avoids woods.

Stanley Alford

This warbler was first discovered wintering in palm habitats in the West Indies. It has no association with palms in North America; it nests in northern bogs and muskeg and, in our region, winters on the ground and in open-country brush. It is a ground-feeding species taking a varied diet of insects, berries and weed seeds. The bird is vocally active while feeding, but the lisping notes are high-pitched and faint and can be confused with those of the slate-colored junco and the chipping sparrow. The rusty cap and yellow eye stripe are easily seen with field glasses, but a behavioral gesture is the most important identifier: the tail bobs up and down constantly. The bright yellow undertail coverts are sometimes exposed on the upstroke, explaining the folk name "yellow tip-up." "Wagtail warbler" is a common name no less descriptive.

Two races of *palmarum* are recognized. The eastern form, which we are most likely to see, is called the yellow palm warbler after its straw yellow underparts. In the western subspecies, the lower belly grades to pale yellow or white, though the undertail coverts and throat retain the rich yellow. Seasonal and geographic variations can also be seen in the eastern race.

COMMON YELLOWTHROAT
Geothlypis trichas

FIELD MARKS: A black mask covers the male's forehead and extends to the neck. A thin white margin separates the mask from the cap. The male's cap, back and wings are olive green; his throat and breast are yellow. The female lacks the mask and is yellow only at the throat; her breast is buff to brown.
LENGTH: 4½ inches.
VOICE: The irritation note given when a human approaches its wintering grounds is a sharp TCHCH. The territorial call is a much-repeated WITCHITY, WITCHITY, WITCHITY.
RANGE IN OUR REGION: Winters in the lower piedmont and coastal plain from southern Virginia to Texas. Nests throughout our region.
HABITAT: Brushy overgrown fields, roadsides, fencerows; often prefers moist and marshy open places.

♂

Walking along a country road or through a weedy field, I often hear a low, twangy note from deep within a briar patch. It sounds like a single pluck on a loose banjo string. Approaching the thicket, I catch a glimpse of yellow and black as a small warbler flits within the tangle, surfacing repeatedly to TCHCH his note of protest and to eye the interloper. I maintain silence. For a few moments we play a game of hide-and-seek in which I see the little warbler just as it flits from view, seemingly caught in a struggle with irritation, curiosity and a desire to escape. Then I make loud swishing and hissing noises, and the bird goes into a rage. He leaps to a high briar and hurls his raspy note in defiance, displaying himself boldly to the source of this outrageous provocation.

I hardly need an unobstructed view of the black mask and yellow underparts to identify the yellowthroat. The irritation note and the peek-a-boo game in the briar patch are distinctive behavior. Easily induced to temper tantrums, the yellowthroat is the most "swishable" bird in our region; the naturalist can always get a response by squeaking or swishing.

The yellowthroat stays within a few feet of the ground, darting through the brush and weeds of fallow fields. It shows a preference for damp places, provided the character of the habitat is basically open and unwooded. Marshes and pond edges are favored, though the bird often occupies dry fields.

In winter yellowthroats concentrate in the southern part of our region, where the temperate climate enables them to indulge their taste for insects even in the coldest months. In spring the males begin their WITCHITY, WITCHITY territorial pronouncement in our latitudes, then explode northward to nest well into Canada. A reduced population nests in our region.

FAMILY ICTERIDAE

EASTERN MEADOWLARK
Sturnella Magna

FIELD MARKS: A black V at the throat against brilliant yellow underparts identifies the meadowlark. The outer tail feathers show white in flight. The upperparts are a quaillike camouflage of mottled brown. The sexes are indistinguishable.
LENGTH: 8½ inches.
VOICE: The song is a joyous, pure-toned whistle.
RANGE IN OUR REGION: Winters and nests throughout.
HABITAT: Fields and meadows under active cultivation, but not abandoned farmland.

Tussocks of grass shelter the meadowlark as it feeds in an open pasture on a warm day in late winter. At our approach the bird crouches in the browned vegetation, exposing only the perfectly camouflaged upper parts of its body. It bursts from the grass on quivering wings and protests our intrusion with a sharp CHEEEEEET. Flashing its white outer tail feathers, the meadowlark arcs upward twenty feet, turns to fly with the wind, then glides away on stiffly set wings. Once or twice more on the escape flight, the stubby, pointed wings alternate between moments of quivering powered flight and brief glides with the tips held slightly downward. The meadowlark flutters to a landing a hundred yards away and stands upright to keep an eye on us.

If we leave his meadow and watch with binoculars from the woods' edge, we may see the meadowlark respond to the season's first warmth by flying to a fence post and singing the welcome message, "Ah, spring is here." The rich, clear notes, whistled with an almost

human quality, ring across the fields as he displays his golden breast in the sunlight.

Though the meadowlark occupies our region in all seasons, it does migrate. Some of the individuals who winter with us nest well into Canada. When the northward movement starts, year-round residents sing vigorously to ward off invaders from the south. Epic battles of song and puffery ensue, occasionally degenerating into vicious scuffles in the air and in the grass. Several males in contest over an available female may put on elaborate displays of aerial pursuit with frantic chattering vocalizations. Intensified meadowlark activity attends the first hints of spring.

The meadowlark's fare in winter consists of weed seeds, wasted grain and insect grubs. During the nesting season, the bird eats vast numbers of insect pests that compete directly with man and his livestock for grass crops.

RED-WINGED BLACKBIRD
Agelaius phoeniceus

FIELD MARKS: The male is solid black with red shoulder patches edged in yellow. The female is brownish with bold brown streaking on the breast.
LENGTH: 7¼ inches.
VOICE: The call is a rich CHUCK. The song, which begins in winter, is a bubbling, musical OAK-A-LEEEE.
RANGE IN OUR REGION: Nests in all sections. Abandons the higher mountain elevations in winter.
HABITAT: Fields, marshes, livestock pens.

The redwing is one of the most numerous birds in the world. Like the common grackle it is a legitimate, not alien, North American species that has benefited greatly from humanity's alterations to the land. Large-scale agriculture has become a principal source of fall and winter food for the redwing, as well as for other gregarious blackbirds including the starling, the brown-headed cowbird and the common grackle. Much of the grain these birds take would otherwise be wasted. Weed seeds and undigested material in livestock manure are also important foods.

In winter redwings gather in large flocks to forage in the fields and barnyards, sometimes mixing with starlings, grackles and cowbirds. Flocks of redwings wheel and turn in tight clusters while individual birds rise and fall within the flock. With the lengthening days of February, males desert the great wintering flocks and claim their breeding territories in ponds and marshes. Gripping a reed or willow twig, the male hunches his shoulders forward to display his crimson epaulets and sings his OAK-A-LEE lovesong. When the females arrive, they must seek the male's permission to nest within his territory, and they must be prepared to incubate their eggs and raise their brood unaided.

First-year males with their brown feather edgings and muted shoulder patches are not attractive to the females and are not tolerated on the territories of mature males. As a result, an excess of available females develops in some localities, and the stronger males become polygamous. In early spring a well-situated male may divide his attentions among as many as five of the sparrow-brown ladies, displaying before each and escorting them on their labors about the territory as they gather nesting material and food. He does not, however, condescend to participate in any domestic effort except the mating act.

Whereas the winter flocks of grackles may reach tens of thousands of individuals, redwings gather in roosts of, literally, millions. These aggregations have been known to kill stands of trees by blanketing the forest floor with their droppings. Huge roosts, mixed but composed mostly of redwings, have been reported recently near Scotland Neck, North Carolina, and in the Great Dismal Swamp in Virginia. Wildlife authorities, responding to the grumblings of farmers and others who consider the flocks a "nuisance," attempt with varying degrees of success to exterminate the birds by spraying the roosts with detergent before a cold rain so that the birds die of exposure. It is this writer's not-particularly-humble opinion that this practice is ill-advised and inhumane no less than the earlier governmental efforts to eliminate the prairie dog, the coyote, the buffalo (the real purpose, of course, was to eliminate the American Indian) and the cougar. Natural controls should be encouraged, because the detergents indiscriminately kill all species of birds, including any owls who are in the roost for the purpose of preying on the blackbirds. Many well-informed observers are convinced, moreover, that the redwing is an overall aid to agriculture because of the vast number of cropland insects it eats during the growing season.

RUSTY BLACKBIRD
Euphagus carolinus

FIELD MARKS: A small blackbird. The male is entirely black but lacks iridescence; the female is brownish gray. The eyes of mature individuals are white (brown to yellow during the first winter). Feathers are edged in rust in the fall.
LENGTH: 8 inches.
VOICE: A high squeak suggesting a rusty gate hinge.
RANGE IN OUR REGION: Winters in all sections except the mountains.
HABITAT: Wooded wetlands.

♂

The rusty blackbird is one of several avian denizens of the moist woodlands who have a counterpart in the open country. As the woodcock and red-shouldered hawk correspond to the snipe and the red-tailed hawk, respectively, the rusty blackbird replaces the redwing where open wet places grade into moist wooded tracts.

I met the rusty blackbird one March day while waiting in a blind from which I was watching a nest of horned owls in College Park, Maryland. A large flock noisily made its way toward my hiding place, individuals leap-frogging ahead of one another, advancing the flock like a black wave across the moist forest floor. Many passed close in front of my blind, allowing me to watch them scratch and pick in the leaf litter for insects and seeds. One of the parent owls arrived at the nest, and the rusties whooshed away through the woods in a tight cloud.

The rusty blackbird gets its name from the brown edgings on the feathers in fall. As winter wears on, the rust becomes less visible, though fuscous flecks can be seen against the mica black of the male's breast at any time on the wintering grounds. The white eye of mature birds is a diagnostic feature differentiating the rusty from the yellow-eyed common grackle. The rusty's tail is slightly longer than the redwing's, but much shorter than the keeled empennage of the grackle.

COMMON GRACKLE
Quiscalus quiscula

FIELD MARKS: A long, slender bird of uniform black. Iridescence on the head, neck and back may appear green, violet or bronze. The bill, typically icterid, is long, thin and pointed; the tail is long and keeled. The female is smaller than the male and is less iridescent. The eyes of mature individuals are yellow.
LENGTH: 10 to 12 inches.
VOICE: The song, which begins in late winter, is a loud, ascending squeak. Winter feeding flocks converse in a low, guttural GAK, GAK.
RANGE IN OUR REGION: Nests in all sections; abandons higher mountain elevations in winter.
HABITAT: Moves freely between woodlands, open fields, residential areas.

One of the impressive wildlife phenomena of autumn is the formation of vast flocks of grackles over their wintering range. Numberless aggregations gather to forage in the woodlands for mast and fruits, then to flow like a winding river to the newly sprouted fields of small grain, which they sometimes damage seriously. Tens of thousands of grackles in a single flock are not an uncommon sight where conditions are favorable, and the spectacle offers us some idea of how the great flights of passenger pigeons must have appeared. The cackling hordes, when feeding, create the sound of a distant waterfall. The commotion shifts suddenly to a low roar when the flock takes flight. Once underway, the grackles add their voices to the rush of their wings, and at close range the sound possesses the powerful, frightening quality of an onrushing thunderstorm.

On several occasions I have seen red-tailed and Cooper's hawks shadowing flocks of grackles in the open fields and woods, respectively. The hawks prob-

♂

ably reason that a few among the vast population of grackles will be sick or inept enough to show a fatal weakness. On another occasion I watched, chagrined, from a boat anchored on a large lake, as an endless river of the "crow blackbirds" approached. A gentle rain of their droppings speckled the water, edging ever nearer as the course of the ribbon of grackles drifted over our moored craft. Unfortunately, the little outboard motor flooded in the hasty attempts to start it just as we found ourselves directly beneath the flowing mass of birdlife.

By late winter the flocks of grackles disperse into smaller courtship groups which later form nesting communes. Amorous males woo their brides by posturing with their bills pointed skyward and uttering the rasping metallic shrieks that have been dubbed the "wheelbarrow chorus."

Though farmers justifiably complain about the depredations of flocks of grackles on their ripening corn and sprouting cover crops, the grackles' varied diet compensates for some of the damage. The species preys heavily upon crop-destroying insects and, surprisingly, upon mice. Grackles strut along the edges of ponds, taking crawfish and small aquatic vertebrates. They vandalize the nests of other birds and may even prey on the adults of some of the smaller birds.

SAVANNAH SPARROW
Passerculus sandwichensis

FIELD MARKS: The heavily streaked breast lacks a central spot; the tail is short and notched. The upperparts vary with locality from pale to dark brown. Black may be present in the streaking on the back. There is a wide yellow or buff line over the eye. The sexes are indistinguishable.
LENGTH: 4¾ inches.
VOICE: Faint musical CHIPs.
RANGE IN OUR REGION: Winters in the piedmont and coastal plain. The wintering range includes roughly the southern half of the United States. The vast nesting range extends from the Great Lakes northward.
HABITAT: Dry, grassy pastures. Prefers short grass.

Savannah and grasshopper sparrows are part of a group known by some as the "short-tailed grass sparrows." It can be said that the favored length of the grass is a major distinction in the ecological niches of the two species: the grasshopper sparrow seeks deep grass cover; the savannah prefers short grasses. The two are easily distinguished by the grasshopper's plain and the savannah's streaked breast. The savannah is more easily confused in our region in winter with the vesper sparrow, the latter being distinguished by its longer tail and white outer tail feathers. Also, it is useful to look for the savannah sparrow's thin white crown stripe.

The savannah sparrow gleans the short grasses in open fields near coastal and marshy areas. It is easily seen wintering in the lawns of coastal towns in our region. Alexander Wilson named the bird in 1811 after discovering it in Savannah, Georgia.

Like the grasshopper sparrow, the savannah prefers to stay close to the ground. When startled, it takes flight for a short distance, returns quickly to earth, and scurries through the grass. On the ground it moves in short sprints, searching for seeds and insects. Beetles are important in its diet.

GRASSHOPPER SPARROW
Ammodramus savannarum

FIELD MARKS: The large, flat head and short, pointed tail are distinctive. Upperparts are varying shades of brown and black interlaced with white or buff. The buff underparts bear no markings. Yellow can sometimes be seen at the wrists. A creamy line divides the crown. The sexes are indistinguishable.
LENGTH: 4½ inches.
VOICE: An insectlike TSICK, TSICK, TSICK.
RANGE IN OUR REGION: Winters in the piedmont and coastal plain from North Carolina southward.
HABITAT: Deserted farmyards, overgrown pastures, open fields with thick fencerows.

The grasshopper sparrow gets its name from its buzzing call, which is said to be an exact mimicry of the stridulation of the meadow grasshopper, *Orchelium vurgare*. The sound is faint and so high-pitched that many parts of it are inaudible to some humans. L. A. Hausman suggests that the call can be reproduced by whispering TSICK, TSICK, TSICK "through closely set teeth."

Grasshoppers are included in the bird's diet, as are a variety of other insects. The grasshopper sparrow relies on a greater year-round percentage of insects for its food than does any other sparrow. It inhabits open pastures and weedy fields where insects abound. Except when sunning and singing its raspy notes, the grasshopper sparrow is busy threading through the thick grasses in search of grasshoppers, crickets, spiders, beetles and other insects and arachnids.

"Quail sparrow" is one of the bird's common names. The markings on the head and upperparts suggest a bobwhite's protective pattern. This is not surprising since both are ground-feeding birds of the same grassy habitat. The grasshopper sparrow also shares the quail's habit of permitting close approach, then bursting from the ground cover in a short, low escape flight. One of the grasshopper sparrow's identifying characteristics is dropping vertically down to friendly cover at the end of its flight.

WHITE-CROWNED SPARROW
Zonotrichia leucophrys

FIELD MARKS: The wide center stripe on the crown is edged boldly in black. The bill is pinkish. The posture is erect. There is no white throat patch. The sexes are indistinguishable.
LENGTH: 6 inches.
VOICE: Varying subdued, fuzzy whistles.
RANGE IN OUR REGION: Winters with us irregularly, most often in the higher elevations of our region.
HABITAT: Shrubs in open spaces.

The white-crowned is often mistaken for the similar white-throated sparrow. The white-crowned's erect posture and white, bristly crest are helpful identifiers. It is principally a western bird who visits our region in modest numbers in winter. Several races are recognized; the eye stripe of the eastern race begins at the eye, whereas that of western races begins at the bill. The head feathers ruffle into a low crest at slight provocation, such as an intrusion into the bird's territory by a birdwatcher making a "swishing" noise.

Research into the homing instincts of white-crowned sparrows shows that they possess extraordinary abilities at long-distance navigation, though the methods they employ are poorly understood. In 1962 more than five hundred white-crowneds were captured near San Jose, California. They were banded and released at the Patuxent Wildlife Research Center in Maryland. Their normal north-south migration route lay thousands of miles to the west. A year later eight of the white-crowneds showed up in San Jose. North-south migrations spanning all of North America are casual jaunts for this bird.

The sighting of a white-crowned sparrow in any locality east of the mountains in the Carolinas is note-worthy; the more southerly the observation in our region, the more unusual it becomes. North into Virginia and Maryland, the white-crowned more commonly winters in the piedmont. It is frequently seen in company with white-throated and song sparrows feeding on berries and weed seeds in fencerows.

SWAMP SPARROW
Melospiza georgiana

FIELD MARKS: Head markings include a rusty cap, dark eye stripe and gray face. The wings, back and tail are dusky; the breast is gray and unmarked. The sexes are indistinguishable.
LENGTH: 5 inches.
VOICE: A metallic CHINK on the wintering grounds. The territorial call is comparable to the chipping sparrow's melodious WIRT, WIRT, WIRT.
RANGE IN OUR REGION: Winters throughout.
HABITAT: Keeps to the open wetlands during winter, but can be found in weedy fields during migration.

The swamp sparrow is as shy and furtive as the winter wren, with whom it shares the wet, overgrown bottomlands in winter. It prefers bushy bogs and avoids forested wetlands. Gaining a clear look at a swamp sparrow can be difficult, for the bird ducks into the shrubbery or scurries like a mouse (or a winter wren) under the topsoil overhangs along streams. A swishing or squeaking sound can peak its curiosity momentarily, but once it identifies the source of the sound as human, the swamp sparrow vanishes into a muddy tussock.

The winter diet is divided approximately equally between animal and vegetable items. Aquatic insects are important in the diet in all seasons except during fall migration, when small groups forage for weed seeds in overgrown fields and gardens. The wetland orientation is strongest in the breeding season, weakest on fall migration, and moderately strong on the wintering grounds. Unforested lowlands near water offer the best chance for a winter sighting, but the swamp sparrow is frequently found in the uplands, mixing with flocks of other sparrows.

Chapter III
Birds of Prey

great horned owl

Vultures, Hawks and Falcons
(Order Falconiformes)

FAMILY CATHARTIDAE

TURKEY VULTURE
Cathartes aura

FIELD MARKS: The entirely black plumage and bare head are diagnostic. The bird soars for extended periods, rarely flapping, holding its wings above the horizontal. The sexes are indistinguishable.
LENGTH: 25 inches.
WINGSPAN: 72 inches.
VOICE: None audible from a distance. Grunts and hisses while competing for carrion or to protest a close approach to the nest.
RANGE IN OUR REGION: Winters and nests throughout.
HABITAT: Soars over all habitats.

From a distance all soaring birds appear black, and distinguishing among them can be difficult. The key to the turkey vulture's identity is the dihedral angle at which the wings are held in flight. The tail extends rearward considerably past the trailing edge of the wings and is usually closed or moderately fanned. In our region turkey vultures often fly in company with black vultures, whose short, fanned tails scarcely protrude aft of the wings. When the larger turkey vulture soars closer, the bare red head is diagnostic.

The upward dihedral helps stabilize the great bird in rough air. When turbulence rocks the turkey vulture, the wing that goes up loses lift while the other wing's lift increases as it approaches the horizontal. This dihedral design is built into most commercial aircraft to gain the same stabilizing effect.

The turkey vulture's wing loading (the ratio of body

weight to wing area) is the lowest of any North American cathartid at 1125 square centimeters of supporting area per pound of body weight. It increases the bird's susceptibility to turbulence and necessitates the dihedral. The advantage gained by low wing loading is an enhanced ability to soar in the slightest updraft. Turkey vultures roosting in the same canyon with the California condor have been observed to begin soaring earlier than the condor as the morning sun warmed the earth and generated increasingly strong thermal currents.

After a few launching wing strokes, the turkey vulture can soar literally all day without flapping. With a yet-unexplained ability to find rising air currents, the

great black glider can seemingly gain or lose altitude at will. I once saw a turkey vulture glide in a straight line to a spot in the sky and abruptly begin circling. Within a few turns it gained hundreds of feet, then glided away in a different direction. A red-tailed hawk came to the same spot in the sky from a third direction and repeated the performance, probably taking its cue from the vulture.

Soaring and gliding in wide sweeps over the countryside, the turkey vulture searches for dead animals. It supplements keen eyesight with a sharp sense of smell and has demonstrated an ability to find a decomposing carcass by smell alone. A theory that the sight of flies and other carrion-associated insects enables the vulture to find its food was put to rest by an experiment involving the release of gasses smelling like carrion—the turkey vultures in the area responded enthusiastically. Examination of its brain shows the turkey vulture's olfactory structures to be three times the size of the black vulture's.

Finding a meal by whatever means, the turkey vulture alights and dines with its kin and with black vultures. It holds the food down with strong feet, removes the eyeballs, then proceeds to dissect carefully the ripe carcass with a long bill suited ideally to the purpose. Noncarrion food includes fish, insects usually taken on or near a carcass, occasionally newborn birds and animals, and a small portion of vegetable matter.

The turkey vulture winters in our region and extends its range northward to the Great Lakes during the breeding season. The nest is a scrape on or near the ground in a hollow log, a cave, a cliff or a thicket. There the turkey vulture feeds its downy chicks lovingly regurgitated chunks of carrion.

BLACK VULTURE
Coragyps atratus

FIELD MARKS: All plumage is black except for the light gray "windows" visible in flight at the base of the primary feathers. The unfeathered head is black. The tail is short and squared and is usually fanned widely in flight. The sexes are indistinguishable.
LENGTH: 24 inches.
WINGSPAN: 54 inches.
VOICE: Hisses and grunts near the nest and while feeding.
RANGE IN OUR REGION: Winters and nests north to Maryland and southern Illinois. Most numerous in the southern part of our region.
HABITAT: Soars over all areas, especially farms and roadsides where dead animals might be found.

It is hard to imagine a less attractive bird than the black vulture seen perched at close range. The naked, black-skinned head with warty wattles, the elongated cere and the weak bill do not inspire human admiration. In flight, however, the "carrion crow" is quick and hawklike, adroitly maneuvering its heavy body and 4½-foot wingspread. In February, 1976, I watched an aerial courtship in which three black vultures alternated leadership through a series of spectacular aerobatics including abrupt turns, "split S's" and dives. They were as agile as ravens.

The black vulture's wing loading is heavier than that of the turkey vulture, and the black must frequently resort to powered flight unless the thermal currents are strong. The increased stability resulting from the relatively high ratio of weight to supporting wing area

permits the black to hold its wings flatter when gliding than can the turkey vulture. The flat wing profile is useful in distinguishing between the two species at a distance.

Coragyps has occasionally been known to eat newborn calves and piglets and has been persecuted widely as a result. There are reports of cattle ranchers in Florida capturing large numbers in baited traps and gassing them en masse with the exhaust of a truck. My own observations have been that black vultures in attendance at the birth of a calf are interested in the placenta rather than the infant. I have watched black vultures wait patiently until the process of birth was completed and the calf was safely suckling before they cleaned up the leftovers.

Gregarious in all seasons, black vultures gather in large roosting flocks in winter and nest in colonies of up to a dozen pairs in spring. Dead trees and power-line trestles are favored roosts; the bird in the photograph above has just left such a perch. Black and turkey vultures sometimes share these roosts, just as they share hunting territories. The black lacks the turkey vulture's ability to find carrion by smell, but clearly benefits from keeping an eye on the larger vulture's hunting success. Black vultures usually prevail over turkey vultures in disputing a carcass.

COOPER'S HAWK
Accipiter cooperii

FIELD MARKS: Coloring includes slate gray upperparts, dark cap and light underparts finely barred with rust and white. The wings are broad and short; the tail is long and *rounded*. Immature birds are streaked with brown. The females are larger than the males.
LENGTH: Male, 16 inches; female, 18½ inches.
WINGSPAN: Male, 28 inches; female, 32 inches.
VOICE: Loud, harsh KAK, KAK, KAK repeated many times.
RANGE IN OUR REGION: Winters and nests throughout.
HABITAT: Open woodlands and wood margins.

The Cooper's is the larger of the two wood hawks occurring regularly in our region. Its rounded tail, at rest and in flight, distinguishes the Cooper's from the smaller sharp-shin, whose tail is square-tipped. The female Cooper's is larger than her mate; the male is only slightly larger than a female sharp-shin. The plumage of mature Cooper's hawks is slate gray above and finely barred with reddish brown on white below. Fine bars following the wing contours are visible from below in flight, and the tail has several wide, distinct bands. Immature birds are brownish above, streaked with brown on white below.

Short, rounded wings and a long tail fit the Cooper's, and the other accipiters, for flying through the woods. The elongated tail gives the added maneuverability needed in chasing small birds through dense forest vegetation. Strong thrusts with the wings held close to the body enable the Cooper's hawk to thread its way swiftly through the trees. In grimly determined pursuit of a victim, the Cooper's audibly batters its wings against limbs and foliage, and even dives into thick brushy undergrowth when necessary to extract a small bird.

This tenacity in pursuit of bird prey earned the Cooper's a bad reputation among poultry keepers in earlier times before the technology of chicken farming went indoors. Nothing short of a well-aimed shotgun blast would stop a Cooper's hawk once it developed a taste for pullets. One story, perhaps apocryphal, but plausible considering the bird's predatory audacity, describes a Cooper's hawk catching a chicken under the skirt of a farmer's wife.

Birds smaller than chickens form the bulk of the Cooper's natural food. A study by Heinz Meng near Ithaca, New York, showed that 80% of the Cooper's hawk's food is bird prey, mainly starlings. Flickers, rusty blackbirds and other forest birds augment the Cooper's fare, as do quail and meadowlarks taken occasionally near the woods' edge.

Fierceness is a characteristic of the accipiter possessed in abundance by the Cooper's. One of the most memorable observations the natural world has offered me involved a male Cooper's hawk defending his nesting territory. Near Hillsborough, North Carolina, in July, 1975, a red-tailed hawk flew across the road, low in front of my car, and I stopped to watch as the big buteo circled and climbed over the adjacent field. The red-tailed wheeled and whistled, riding a thermal air current. Perhaps inadvertently, his circling and soaring carried him over a small promontory of deciduous woods. Bursting from the forest canopy in a fury of vocal threats, the Cooper's hawk climbed to attack the much larger red-tail. I watched as the accipiter made repeated passes at the soaring hawk, on two occasions doubling back quickly after a near miss to strike from the rear. For long minutes the hawks screamed as they dueled above the trees until the larger bird set its wings and sped away toward its open field habitat. The victorious Cooper's continued to call and circle above the woodlot, now his beyond dispute.

SHARP-SHINNED HAWK
Accipiter striatus

FIELD MARKS: Distinguishing features include slate gray upperparts, light underparts finely barred with rust and white, and a dark cap on a flat head. The wings are broad and short, the tail long and *square-tipped*. Immature birds are streaked with brown. The female is considerably larger than the male.
LENGTH: Male, 11 inches; female, 13 inches.
WINGSPAN: Male, 21 inches; female, 30 inches.
VOICE: Short series of KAK, KAK, KAK notes and a thin, high, screaming KREEE, KREEE.
RANGE IN OUR REGION: Winters throughout. Abandons coastal plain south of Norfolk, Virginia, in nesting season.
HABITAT: Open woodlands (prefers conifers), fencerows, thickets and farming country.

The sharp-shinned is a scaled-down version of the Cooper's hawk with a single distinguishing feature, its square-cut tail. The color schemes and—with the exception of the shape of the tail—the silhouettes in flight and at rest are nearly identical for the two species. The sexes are similar in plumage, but the female is noticeably larger than the male, as is the case with the two other North American accipiters. The female sharp-shinned is nearly as large as the male Cooper's. Because it is difficult to judge accurately the size of a distant bird, the tail shape should be seen clearly in order to differentiate the sharp-shinned from the Cooper's.

Like the Cooper's, the sharp-shinned preys chiefly on birds. The sharp-shin, however, hunts the open and partially open areas, prudently leaving the deep forest to the Cooper's. Cardinals, sparrows and other open-country birds up to the size of pigeons comprise 70%

of the sharp-shin's diet. Large insects and small mammals make up the balance.

The falcons, who also prey principally on birds, strike from the sky, while the accipiters take birds from the ground, from perches and in fair chase. The sharp-shin hunts mostly songbirds, pursuing flocks of them and matching their every maneuver, principally taking the sluggish or inept individuals. The little "bullet hawk" speeds along fencerows, keeping close to cover, or passes quickly through a suburban backyard containing a bird feeder, hoping to surprise an inattentive songbird. Some friends told me of watching a sharp-shin grab an evening grosbeak from their feeder and fly to a nearby tree to pluck it. Another friend, an experienced birder, watched a male "sharpie" labor past carrying a cardinal almost as large as himself. I remember being nearly overrun by a stampede of fear-crazed robins hotly pursued by a sharp-shin who, herself, flew within a few feet of my head. Several times a year, in all seasons, I hear a fearful silence grip the birdlife in my yard in Carrboro, North Carolina, as a sharp-shin passes through, ever on the lookout for a careless starling or a sluggish sparrow. I especially enjoy recalling the time a sharp-shin attacked a mixed flock of waxwings and robins feeding in a black gum near my garden. The little hunter made no kill but perched and glared at me, giving me a rare opportunity to study in detail a wild and free raptor at close range.

In September thousands of sharp-shins quit the northern part of their nesting range and migrate into our region. The raptors can be seen in great numbers at such "funneling points" along the migration routes as Hawk Mountain, Pennsylvania, and Cape May, New Jersey. The bird is common throughout our region, though it is never numerous in the sense that songbirds are. It is most easily seen here in winter, when the resident sharp-shins are joined by individuals from the north. Breeding pairs defend a territory approximately one mile in diameter, and they nearly always nest in conifers.

♀

MARSH HAWK
Circus cyaneus

FIELD MARKS: The male has steel gray upperparts and is whitish beneath. The female is a nearly uniform brown above and below and shows contoured barrings under the wings in flight. Both sexes have an owllike facial disc and a conspicuous white rump patch. The wings are held above the horizontal in gliding flight.
LENGTH: Male, 18 inches; female, 21 inches.
WINGSPAN: Male, 42 inches; female, 48 inches.
VOICE: The varied utterances include a high, piping PEEP, and short, cackling notes.
RANGE IN OUR REGION: Winters throughout; nests to the north and west of our region.
HABITAT: Open fields, salt and freshwater marshes, old pastures.

A brownish bird courses low over a weedy field; the white "snowball" at the base of its tail holds the observer's attention. The long, slender, rounded wings move through a few easy strokes, then stop well above the horizontal, pigeonlike, as if to keep the primary feathers out of the broom sedge. The long tail suddenly fans downward as a brake, and the bird drops to the ground. It dances a short distance on long, agile legs as it pursues a meadow mouse, pounces and gulps the prey. For a few minutes after feeding, the raptor rests on the ground, then resumes its low hunting patrol, quartering the open fields with sweep after sweep.

That behavior and appearance belong unmistakably to the marsh hawk, the only North American harrier. The long, slender wings and low wing loading (the ratio of body weight to wing area) aptly suit the marsh hawk for sustained powered flight. No other hawk in our region flies so near the ground for such extended periods. The marsh hawk has been observed to fly without resting for half a day at a time. When resting, it often uses the ground and rarely selects a perch higher than a fence post. Only on its long migratory flights does it attain significant altitude.

The marsh hawk, or "hen harrier" as the European race is known, nests to the north of our region, so we do not get to see the spectacular nuptial aerobatics of the ash gray male who has been seen to loop-the-loop continuously for half an hour. His mate watches from the ground or joins him in a series of swooping dives.

Wintering in our region, marsh hawks sometimes gather at dusk in communal roosts on the ground in open fields. One devoted observer of North American birds of prey, Dean Amadon of the American Museum of Natural History, remembers: "I recall one evening visiting a weedy, snow-covered field near the Delaware River. Toward dusk, marsh hawks began to come in singly from various directions with their low, irregular flight. I saw 25 or 30 settle to rest on the ground, sheltered from the chill wind by the dead vegetation. At the same time the "night shift," short-eared owls roosting in that very field, began flying out on their hunting patrols. The field mice had no respites day or night." The marsh hawks would leave the roost in the morning to return by the most direct route to their individual hunting territories as far as five miles away.

The tireless coursing over the fields and wetlands produces a varied diet for the marsh hawk including small mammals, birds, large insects, reptiles, amphibians and fish.

SUBFAMILY BUTEONINAE

RED-TAILED HAWK
Buteo jamaicensis

FIELD MARKS: The tail is uniformly reddish above, light brown below. Bands are visible across the juvenile's tail. The wings and underparts seen from beneath appear whitish with a rusty brown band across the chest. A black edging outlines the underside of the wing. A dark marking extends down the side of the neck and may cover the throat. The amount of dark on the underparts is highly variable. The sexes are indistinguishable.
LENGTH: 18 inches.
WINGSPAN: 48 inches.
VOICE: A loud, screaming KEE-AAHHRR.
RANGE IN OUR REGION: Winters and nests throughout.
HABITAT: Soars over open fields. Roosts and nests in woods.

The red-tail is the largest and most common soaring hawk in our region. It perches for long periods atop a utility pole or dead snag, resting and watching for prey on the ground. On its hunting perch, the red-tail is recognized at a distance by the whitish front, erect posture and broad, thick body. From the rear, the rusty tail hangs conspicuously from beneath the brown back and wings.

With eyesight many times keener than man's, the red-tail spots a cotton rat running between two clumps of broom sedge a hundred yards away. The big buteo leaps into the wind and thrusts a few times with its broad wings, then catches an updraft for a free ride. Arriving over its quarry, the hawk plummets to earth,

seizes the rat, and returns to its perch to dine, preen and rest.

The red-tail is a soaring bird with broad, rounded wings and slotted primary flight feathers adapted for riding the currents of air rising from the surface as a result of the sun's warmth. It wheels in wide circles, easily gaining hundreds of feet of altitude without flapping a wing. On clear winter days, we see the red-tail's whitish underparts as it soars effortlessly above us, and occasionally we catch a glimpse of the red upper tail shining in the sun as the hunter of the open spaces banks to turn.

The red-tail's diet has often—and unfairly—been called into question by poultry owners. Rodents are the staple food source for the red-tail, and a hawk hanging around a hen house is much more likely watching for grain-thieving rats than for chickens. A frequently employed hunting technique is to follow a mowing machine or combine around a field at a discreet distance to grab the small mammals exposed by the harvesting process. Snakes, poisonous and nonpoisonous, are frequent prey of the red-tail. The hawk alights near the snake, dances before it with outstretched wings until the reptile tires from striking, then pounces and closes the talons on the snake's neck. A red-tail's nest in Florida was found to contain three diamond-backed rattlesnakes, one of which was still alive, nearly causing the observer to leap forty feet to the ground. Another brood of red-tailed hawks was raised almost entirely on gopher tortoises. Carrion forms a small portion of the diet, and chicken parts recovered from red-tails' pellets (the regurgitated wads of undigestible matter) may well have been the result of scavenging.

Individuals in the northern part of the red-tail's

range migrate southward in winter, but most of those who nest in our region reside with us the year round. Pairs do not seem to defend their wintering territories against migrants, but they are quick to take offense at a territorial intrusion once the mating season starts. The nuptial aerobatics include crisscrossing flight paths and steep dives, all accompanied by lengthy squeals which suggest the hiss of escaping steam. Pairs build nests of sticks high in the crowns of deciduous trees, decorate them with coniferous sprigs, and tend to reuse them year after year. Light and dark color phases occur in different parts of the red-tail's very large range. The plumages in any area are extremely variable, but red-tails of the southeastern United States are generally light in color. The chocolate chin and throat of the bird in the photograph make it one of the more darkly marked individuals. In all regions the juveniles are banded above and below and lack the red upper tail surface.

RED-SHOULDERED HAWK
Buteo lineatus

FIELD MARKS: Tall and slender when perched. The upperparts are dark brown with dark barring on the wings and rusty shoulder patches. The lower parts are pale brownish red under the head and on the chest, with whitish barring on the lower breast and thighs. Perched and in flight the bird has a dark appearance. Light and dark bands alternate in the wings and tail. The sexes are indistinguishable.
LENGTH: 17 inches.
WINGSPAN: 40 inches.
VOICE: A short, loud KEE-OW repeated several times.
RANGE IN OUR REGION: Winters and nests throughout.
HABITAT: Low, damp woods; wooded stream valleys, farming country.

The red-shouldered hawk is the second most common soaring hawk in our region after the red-tailed. When perched, it appears darker and more slender than the red-tail and often leans forward on its perch. In flight the alternating "windows" and dark bands in the tail and wings are diagnostic. The reddish shoulder patches can be seen under favorable conditions at rest and in flight but should not be considered the primary means of identification.

Being slightly smaller than the red-tailed, the red-shouldered hawk is adapted for woodland living. It surveys its hunting grounds from perches in dead snags and in the crowns of living conifers. The red-shoulder soars above the woodlands and clearings and dives after its prey. The principal fare is woodland rodents, a staple augmented with frogs, snakes, lizards, rabbits and birds as large as crows.

The courtship of the red-shouldered hawk is par-

ticularly noisy. The pairs cavort in the updrafts, then dive into the wetland forest canopy of their nesting habitat to continue the merry chase at full cry. The KEE-YAR, KEE-YAR resounds through the woodlands as the red-shoulders career through the forest with amazing agility. Blue jays sometimes join in the festivities by imitating the red-shoulder's call, but there is a respectful note in the mockery.

Pairs of red-shoulders stay mated for several seasons, perhaps for life. They frequently reuse a nesting site for some years, sometimes building two or more nests in the same or nearby trees for use in alternate years. The architecture of red-shoulders is similar to that of other North American buteos, and these congeners will sometimes use one another's nests. One such platform of sticks in Massachusetts was used successively by pairs of broad-winged, red-tailed and red-shouldered hawks.

The red-shouldered hawk bears a loosely defined ecological relationship to neighboring birds of prey. It hunts the same prey in the same habitat as does the barred owl, taking over from the owl at daybreak. It shares the woods also with the Cooper's hawk but takes different prey—mostly ground-dwelling mammals, whereas the Cooper's' main interest is birds. And the red-shoulder assumes the same rodent-controlling responsibilities for the woodlands that are the red-tail's in the open spaces.

The camera catches this red-shouldered hawk in an unusual position; the head is cocked skyward and the legs are crossed.

FAMILY FALCONIDAE

AMERICAN KESTREL
(Formerly Sparrow Hawk)
Falco sparverius

FIELD MARKS: The male has slate blue wings and crown contrasting with a reddish back and tail. A collar of vertical black stripes rings the neck. The underparts are whitish with black spots. The female's rusty back and tail are barred with black. Her cinnamon underparts are streaked with dark brown, and her head markings are similar to the male's but more subdued.
LENGTH: 9 to 11 inches.
WINGSPAN: 21 inches.
VOICE: Sharp KILLY, KILLY, KILLY.
RANGE IN OUR REGION: Winters throughout; nests in northern portions.
HABITAT: Open country; often seen on utility wires.

The blue-jay-sized kestrel is the smallest North American falcon and is the only one numerous enough to be called common. It is also the most colorful bird of prey on the continent, by a wide margin. The exquisitely colored male wears aqua on his head and wings and rich reddish brown on his crown, back and tail. Two vertical black markings bracket the white cheeks, and a black crescent decorates the nape. Several small owls, including the ferruginous and the pygmy, have similar dark markings at the back of the neck, perhaps useful in warning off larger raptors. A wide, black band occurs just inside the white edging of the male's tail. The female lacks the blue markings and the white on the breast and tail. Her colors are subdued and more uniformly rusty. Still, she is anything but drab by raptor standards.

Three other falcons that can be seen in our region

♂

are the peregrine, the merlin and the gyrfalcon (pronounced jer-falcon). All are rare birds, and, whether or not they are on the official list of rare and endangered species, the future of all three is very much in question. The kestrel's contrastingly healthy populations might be attributed to its adaptability to human civilization and to its generalized feeding habits. Whereas the larger falcons prey almost entirely on birds taken on the wing, the sparrow hawk, in spite of its name, eats a variety of insects, birds and small mammals and reptiles. The kestrel has clearly benefited from the creation through agriculture of more of its favored open-country habitat. The installation of utility wires has created endless miles of perches ideally suited to the tiny raptor's hunting technique.

In fall and winter the kestrel's chunky, handsome form is a frequent sight on roadside wires. The relatively large head makes the silhouette easily distinguishable from that of doves and other wire-perching birds. The kestrel carefully scans the ground for any of its varied items of prey which range in size from grasshoppers to wood rats, the insects comprising over half of the diet. It eats the smallest items on the ground but usually returns to the perch with rodents and birds after breaking the neck with its notched beak.

The kestrel's flight is swift and darting. The wings are long and pointed and are held in a swept-back attitude, though not so steeply as those of the larger, faster falcons. It appears to impact against its landing perches at greater-than-prudent speed, necessitating a pronounced dip of the long tail for balance. When something on the ground attracts a flying kestrel's interest, the little falcon turns into the wind and hovers watchfully on shallow wingbeats. The plunging strike from a hover is an exciting and readily observable vignette from nature's drama.

♀

Owls *(Order Strigiformes)*

Family Strigidae

SCREECH OWL
Otus asio

FIELD MARKS: A small owl whose streaked, mottled plumage occurs in brown, red and gray phases. The ear tufts are prominent. The eyes are yellow. The sexes are indistinguishable.
LENGTH: 8 inches.
VOICE: A lengthy, tremulous wail of even or descending tone.
RANGE IN OUR REGION: Nests and winters throughout.
HABITAT: Woodlands, farm country encompassing orchards and woodlots.

The low, tremulous whistle of this little owl drifts mysteriously through the forest on spring and summer nights, troubling the sleep of country folk and townspeople alike. "Death owl" is one of its common names; the eerie call presages the hearer's death, according to superstition, unless preventive steps are taken, such as getting out of bed to turn over a shoe or pull out a trouser pocket. Whereas the effect may be "spooky," the smoothly warbled tremolo of this bird, misnamed for an Old World congener, is anything but a screech. For me the voice is a gentle reminder of soft summer nights from my childhood, when I heard the happy call of a night creature above the soft hum of an old electric fan.

The screech owl's winter food consists mostly of small rodents and a few birds. In summer the diet includes a high percentage of insects, many of which are picked off in flight. Luna moths and cicadas are popular prey of screech owls.

The screech owl spends its winters alone and silent. Individuals in the northern reaches of the breeding range drift southward in the coldest months when territories are guarded loosely, if at all, but most spend the year in the same general area. The days are spent sleeping in a semi-torpor in a natural tree cavity or woodpecker hole. I remember gently lifting a possum-playing screech owl from a wood duck's nesting box one day for a close inspection. It sat in my palm with its eyes narrowed to slits and made no effort to escape. A scientist once weighed a screech owl by lifting it off its perch with the scale hooked under its bill. Screech owls can endure weeks of foul winter weather without hunting by continuing the energy-saving torpor night and day, perhaps occasionally eating some stored food.

Although docile while roosting on winter days, the screech owl becomes a "feathered wildcat" in defense of its nest. Any animals, humans included, are subject to attack if they show unwelcome interest in the nesting cavity. Urban dwellers are sometimes assaulted in parks while walking beneath a tree containing a nest.

GREAT HORNED OWL
Bubo virginianus

FIELD MARKS: A massive, blunt-headed bird with prominent ear tufts, yellow eyes and a whitish bib. The upperparts are mottled grays and browns, the underparts lighter and finely barred. A facial disc is evident. The sexes are indistinguishable.
LENGTH: 20 inches.
WINGSPAN: 55 inches.
VOICE: Male, a quick cadence of five or six hoots; female, seven or eight hoots of lower pitch.
RANGE IN OUR REGION: Winters and nests throughout.
HABITAT: All wooded habitats from coastal maritime shrub to highest mountains.

This is our largest owl and, next to the eagles, the mightiest bird of prey in the western hemisphere. If any raptor could justifiably be called dangerous, it would be the great horned owl, for no animal, man included, is immune to this fierce bird's attack. Assaults on humans are rare and are generally prompted by defense of the nest or are directed in error at a fur hat, but the effects can be injurious. A strike to the unprotected head of someone climbing a tree to a nest can cause a serious fall.

The immense natural range of the horned owl suggests something of its adaptability. It is found throughout the Americas wherever trees grow, from the stunted willows of the arctic tundra to the equatorial rain forests and southward to the wind-tortured trees of Tierra del Fuego. Within this range the horned owl hunts in nearly every habitat, including suburban and even urban areas. Its populations appear to be at a maximum in most regions, despite drastic alterations to its habitats and direct persecution by man.

Wherever it lives, the horned owl takes the most readily available prey. Mammal fare ranges from mice and voles to stray cats, small dogs and full-grown foxes. Skunks are regular prey, and even porcupines are sometimes taken, though such an encounter can be fatal to the owl. Among a group of pellets I once collected was one containing the remains of a star-nosed mole, the first reported as prey of a horned owl. Reptiles, amphibians and even fish are in the diet of the great raptor. A careful analysis of pellets collected by Drs. Frank and John Craighead in their Michigan study area showed that rats and mice comprise over 90% of the winter food of horned owls.

I have found evidence that birds are favored as food for the young. At the base of a tree with a nest that I observed in Maryland in 1970, the remains of prey, presumably eaten by the young, contained a much higher proportion of bird bones and feathers than did the pellets of the adults. In Chapel Hill, North Carolina, in 1975, I discovered a nest in a wooded park and found the ground for yards around the nest littered with pigeon feathers. The owls lived in the woods but apparently roamed the town at night, nabbing pigeons from their roosts on University buildings and church steeples. One pellet recovered a few yards from the nest contained the entire leg and talon of a barred owl. The foot had not been subjected to the digestive juices of the horned owl's stomach, so I am left to assume that the bird went about for some time with the smaller owl's foot sticking out of its mouth.

The horned owl's annual cycle is shifted a full season ahead of the schedule of most other birdlife. In midwinter the territorial vocalizations of mated pairs boom across the icy nights. Until recently I lived at the edge of a large wooded tract near Chapel Hill and at times heard as many as three pairs of horned owls defining their boundaries. One pair often called from a tree

over my roof in a fuguelike cadence in which the female boomed in with her lower-voiced sequence at the male's third note.

By Christmas, in the Carolinas, the territories are established and nesting activities begin. The nest is often a remodeled hawk or squirrel dwelling thirty feet or higher in a tree. Both adults share incubation duties, and the young hatch in mid-February. The owlets wear white down for their first fortnight, then grow a brownish coat of down-tipped contour feathers. They eat voraciously while growing. The availability of bird prey on exposed roosting perches before the leaves erupt may be one incentive for early nesting. The fact that the young owls need several months of parental subsidy after fledging in April contributes to the requirement for their early start. Showing the young fledged before the red maple's floral buds open, the photograph underscores the great horned owl's early nesting cycle. Most birds do not begin to nest until after the foliage deploys. Throughout the summer and into autumn the adults feed the young as they learn to hunt for their own prey.

The horned owl is wary but quite comfortable near civilization. Its boldness and its capability as a predator, sometimes of songbirds and small game, led some to consider *virginianus* a "bad" owl. It was not until recently that North Carolina, for example, accorded the horned owl and the Cooper's hawk, another "bad" raptor, the full protection of law. This trend in protection recognizes the new understanding that "good" and "bad" have no meaning in nature, and at best reflect only man's perceived economic interests. The great horned owl is a legitimate predator entitled to its prey no less than the human hunter. It is a necessary controller of rodents in the woods and fields and a benefactor to game, weeding out the sick and inept.

BARRED OWL
Strix varia

FIELD MARKS: The back is brownish with white spotting. The breast is barred, the abdomen striped. Black eyes are set within a pronounced facial disc. The rounded head has no ear tufts. The sexes are indistinguishable.

LENGTH: 18 inches.

WINGSPAN: 44 inches.

VOICE: Two sets of four hoots with an AWW syllable appended to the last hoot. HOOT–HOOT–HOOT–HOOT——HOOT–HOOT–HOOT–HOO–AWW. A colloquial rendering goes, "Who'll cook for you? Who'll cook for you all?"

RANGE IN OUR REGION: Winters and nests throughout.

HABITAT: Wooded swamps and river bottoms, less numerous in upland woods.

This female barred owl was photographed seconds after she left the nest. Her brood patch is clearly visible. This bald spot at the center of the breast is richly supplied with blood at the surface and warms the eggs. Birds' brood patches are rarely visible.

The barred owl is the commonly labeled "hoot owl" of the southern swamps and forests. Its range extends from Canada to Guatemala, with the greatest population densities of the United States found in our region. The barred is a medium-sized owl recognized by its smooth, rounded, unhorned head and by the horizontal barring across the breast. We are much more likely to hear the bird than to see it, so vocal identification is important. The hoots are given in two distinct sets of four with a trailing AWW note on the last hoot. Sometimes a barred owl's single, loud, drawn-out HOO–AWWW shatters the darkness, and the bird

occasionally emits a demonic hissing scream. Sounds resembling the spitting of a bobcat and the barking of a dog are attributed to the barred owl. And one must be prepared to hear these unnerving sounds on an overcast day as well as in the dark of night.

This owl has a wetland orientation in much of our region, preferring to hunt at night in the same wooded bottomlands and swamps that the red-shouldered hawk patrols by day. It prefers mature forests, but frequently visits open spaces.

The barred owl's diet reflects its riparian inclinations. Frogs, fish and crayfish are common items of food for barred owls dwelling near ponds and streams. Small mammals and birds are also important prey. Smaller owls such as the saw-whet and the screech sometimes fall prey to the medium-sized barred, who, in turn, occasionally has an unfavorable encounter with the master of the darkness, the great horned owl. (*See* p. 107.)

The well-developed facial disc associated with the hearing apparatus suggests the barred owl's nocturnal nature. Feathers at the edges of the disc are connected to the flaps of skin which control the very large ear openings, helping the owl focus its hearing and determine the location of the source of a sound. Diurnal owls, such as the burrowing and the snowy, rely less on their hearing as an aid in finding prey, and consequently, they lack the facial disc. One hawk, the marsh hawk, has developed an owllike disc because it hunts by flying close to the ground and relies somewhat on its hearing to detect prey.

The barred owl's hearing is so acute that it is one of the owls known to capture prey in total darkness by sound alone. Under normal hunting conditions of near-darkness, the hearing is used in conjunction with the bird's exceptionally keen night vision. The eyes collect light a hundred times more efficiently than do human eyes. The barred owl can find and kill a wood rat by sight in light equivalent to that of a candle 1170 feet away.

Perching Birds *(Order Passeriformes)*

Family Laniidae

LOGGERHEAD SHRIKE
Lanius ludovicianus

FIELD MARKS: The black mask across the front and sides of the face separates the white throat and underparts from the gray cap and back. The wings and tail appear black at rest; white shows in them in flight. The beak is hooked. The sexes are indistinguishable.
LENGTH: 9 inches.

VOICE: A harsh CHOREE, assorted unmusical squeaks and nasal notes.
RANGE IN OUR REGION: Winters and nests throughout.
HABITAT: Roadside wires, open farm country.

A mockingbird perched on a roadside wire is not an uncommon sight. Occasionally, while birdwatching from a car, we find one who holds its tail nearly horizontal and whose steel gray back is clearly separated from the white underparts. At close range we see a black mask which includes the eyes and passes across the forehead. These are the markings of the loggerhead shrike, called by some the "French mockingbird." Evidence suggests, however, that it is more a case of the mockingbird mimicking the shrike's appearance. The mockingbird may gain some of its dooryard truculence by resembling the fearsome "butcherbird."

The shrike is not particularly tolerant of humans. If a car stops before one perched on a wire, it swoops to within a few feet of the ground and flies straight to an alternate perch, perhaps to a bare snag nearby. The shallow arc of the wing strokes, which are too rapid to count, is outlined by the white markings at the base of the primary feathers. The mockingbird shows similar wing markings, but the wings move through deep, slow, rowing strokes.

From its perch on a snag, the shrike spies a sparrow feeding near the ground a hundred yards distant. The white arcs again trace a low, swift course straight toward the unwitting quarry. Does the sparrow think it is being approached by a cantankerous but harmless mockingbird? It recognizes the shrike too late and heads for cover. The butcherbird pursues the sparrow relentlessly, overtaking it in a thicket. The kill is not so quick as that of a sharp-shin or a screech owl, for the shrike's talons are weak, and it must hammer out the victim's life with its hooked beak.

Laboring into the air with a kill nearly half its size, the shrike heads for a nearby honey locust tree. It impales the sparrow on a thorn, enlarging the grim collection in its larder tree. With the prey firmly secured, the butcherbird slashes with its beak and tugs away bite-sized chunks. If the meal is too generous, it will be finished at a later sitting.

The prey might have been nearly any small bird, rodent or reptile, or any large insect. Grasshoppers are a staple in summer, but in winter, when insects are scarce, the shrike turns to vertebrates.

Authorities describe the loggerhead shrike's status as "uncommon." On their roadside perches, however, the birds are easily spotted, and several may be seen in an hour's drive in many parts of our region. Pairs of shrikes often nest in the same vicinity in which they winter, building a bulky nest of twigs in a small tree in an open field.

Chapter IV
Rare and Uncommon Birds

immature peregrine falcon

Vultures, Hawks and Falcons *(Order Falconiformes)*

FAMILY ACCIPITRIDAE

BALD EAGLE
Haliaeetus leucocephalus

FIELD MARKS: The head and tail of a mature individual are white, the body is brown, and the bill and talons are yellow. Immature birds are a uniform grayish brown with a black bill and gray cere. The sexes are indistinguishable.

LENGTH: 32 to 36 inches.

WINGSPAN: 80 inches.

VOICE: Rapid, sharp notes suggesting those of a guinea fowl.

RANGE IN OUR REGION: Rare and local along coastlines and at a few inland lakes.

HABITAT: Large swamps and coastal marshes, lakes, rivers; always found near water.

With its snowy white head and tail contrasting with its uniformly brown body, the mature bald eagle is unmistakable. In flight the eagle's wings, spanning nearly seven feet, are held flat. When perched, the great bird sits erect, displaying its astonishingly large body and gleaming white head and tail. The head, of course, is not bald; when the eagle was named, the term meant white. The bird is native and peculiar to North America.

Immature bald eagles are less readily identified at a distance because they lack the white head and tail. The uniform coloration is grayer than that of the adult and results in confusion with the turkey vulture and the golden eagle. At a distance, the flat wing profile distinguishes the bald eagle from the dihedral-winged turkey vulture. The immature golden eagle has white under the wings and tail, which the young bald eagle lacks, and the mature golden eagle has a yellow beak

proportionately smaller than the immature bald's black beak. The white head and tail begin to develop in the bald eagle's fourth year, and fully mature plumage is attained by the sixth year of life.

The bald eagle became our national emblem by act of Congress in 1782 over Benjamin Franklin's objections that it is "a bird of bad moral character . . . who does not get his living honestly" (a reference probably to the eagle's preference for robbing ospreys of their catch when possible) and "like those among men who live by sharping and robbing . . . is generally poor and very often lousy."

Though honored as a symbol of a nation's strength and courage, the bald eagle spent the next 158 years as a fair target for gunners seeking amusement or vengeance for alleged depredations. The National Emblem Law of 1940 protected the bald eagle in the then forty-eight states but left the bird open to persecution in Alaska, where the largest populations of the species reside. The Alaska legislature, responding to the concerns of fishermen, declared a bounty on the bald eagle that was ultimately paid on over a hundred thousand victims before its repeal in 1952. Even with strict modern protection, an occasional cretinous vandal succumbs to the temptation to "bring low the mighty," and another eagle is surreptitiously shot. In 1970 the nation was horrified to learn that sheep ranchers had conspired to massacre more than five hundred bald and golden eagles by shotgunning them from helicopters over public lands.

As would be expected, ignorance is central to the persecution of this magnificent bird, for a rudimentary understanding of its feeding habits would allay most concerns regarding depredations on commercial fish, lambs and human infants left unattended in baby carriages. The bald eagle's diet averages 80% fish, mostly dead or dying, and 20% carrion. One of its favored hunting practices is to perch downstream from a hydroelectric plant and feast on chunks of fish killed in the turbines.

Only five thousand individuals of the southern race remain in the forty-eight contiguous states, and that race is clearly in danger of extinction. Fortunately the Alaskan, or northern, race is not thought to be endangered. In our region the bald eagle is extremely rare, and the outlook for the few remaining individuals is bleak. In 1975, a total of forty-six young were produced in the Chesapeake Bay area, which was once the eagle's principal breeding stronghold north of Florida. There are perhaps three eyries still active along the coast of South Carolina. The last known nesting in North Carolina was recorded at Lake Mattamuskeet in 1971. In 1974 the refuge manager at Mattamuskeet reported hearing the chief of a logging crew say that his men had cut a tree containing an eagle's nest, probably somewhere in Dare County. The oversight is difficult to understand because an eagle's nest is reused year after year, and the accumulated nesting material, weighing as much as two tons, becomes a prominent part of the landscape. At any rate, the immense swampy forest that provided the eagle's nesting habitat was leveled recently to make way for a "superfarm."

Though our region supports precious few bald eagle nests, largely because of the destruction of habitat and the poisoning of the environment with agricultural insecticides, we may still make an occasional sighting. Eagles establish favored fishing spots and tend to use them for weeks on end. In 1975, to the delight of hundreds who saw them, four bald eagles wintered in the vicinity of the dam at Kerr Lake in North Carolina.

OSPREY
Pandion haliaetus

FIELD MARKS: The wings are crooked in flight. Markings feature white underparts and head, black mask and blackish upperparts. There is streaking on the crown of the slightly larger female.
LENGTH: 22 inches.
WINGSPAN: 5 to 6 feet.
VOICE: High, piping PEEPs.
RANGE IN OUR REGION: Winters occasionally along the Georgia and South Carolina coasts, marshes and sounds. Ventures inland in late winter and early spring as northward migration begins.
HABITAT: Near water. Inland, it favors large farm ponds and rivers. Greatest concentrations are in coastal marshes and sounds.

By every appearance, the osprey is a hawk. The hooked beak, the profile of the head, the slotted primary feathers and the heavy talons leave no doubt. A single feature, the rotating outer toe, earns the osprey a place in a family separate from all other hawks, though some students of birdlife believe that a subfamily within the Accipitridae would be more appropriate.

The outer toe can be rotated, owllike, to the rear of the foot to help the osprey hold its slithery prey which consists almost entirely of fish. Thorny spicules on the pads of the feet aid in gripping. Once the talons are fastened into the fish, they are clenched securely by the geometry of the leg bones and tendons. Ospreys occasionally bind to fish so large that the prey drowns the "fish hawk." Fishermen's nets have yielded osprey skeletons still grappling with the fatal fish.

Usually the osprey prevails. The big bird hovers thirty feet or so above the water, aims, then folds its wings and dives headlong and feetfirst after the fish. No other bird enters the water with its head aimed at the target and its feet preceding the head. Rising to the surface with its prize, the fish hawk labors into the air with deep wing strokes and streamlines the fish into the wind, usually holding near the head with the left talon and gripping the body with the right. When safely airborne, the osprey shakes the water from its body as would a hound after crossing a stream. It flies to a feeding perch and, pinning the meal to a limb with its talons, tears off bite-sized chunks. The debris of gills, heads and fins beneath the favorite feeding tree of an osprey who visits a pond near Chapel Hill each spring draws an army of flies and scavengers.

The fish hawk has few natural enemies, though it is subject to the piracy of the bald eagle. Like the osprey, our national bird dines principally on fish. Where it shares a territory with an osprey, the eagle occasionally attacks the smaller raptor, forcing it to drop its catch. In a few quick wing strokes the eagle neatly catches the loot, and the osprey must fish again.

Ospreys have more to contend with than occasional skyjackings by lazy eagles. North American man has long amused himself by taking potshots at ospreys from excursion boats and more recently has so befouled the environment with poisons that the fish hawk's ability to reproduce has all but collapsed. Like the bald eagle, the osprey ingests chemical pesticides concentrated in the flesh of the fish it eats, with the result that mating and nesting behavior becomes indifferent, and eggs are laid with paper-thin shells within which embryonic ospreys fail to develop. Populations have fallen drastically in the past few years. The loose nesting colonies along the coastal waters of our region have been decimated, and a pair of nesting ospreys is now a rare sight. Two eyries that I observed for several years on Chincoteague Island, Virginia, have been unattended since 1973.

Hopes for the fish hawk rest on the ability of its prey to purge themselves of the now-outlawed DDT and other hydrocarbon pesticides, but poisons applied to the land a decade ago may only now be reaching the fish. Indicators show that the osprey continues to slip toward oblivion. Interested naturalists watching the farm ponds and tidal creeks of our region will be among the first to witness the osprey's recovery, if it occurs.

FAMILY FALCONIDAE

PEREGRINE FALCON
Falco peregrinus

FIELD MARKS: The back and wings of the male are slate gray, those of the female dusky brown. The breast and under surface of the wings are white finely barred with brown. A dark cap and moustachial stripes decorate the head.
LENGTH: Male, 17 inches; female, 19 inches.
WINGSPAN: About 40 inches.
VOICE: Shrill, screaming notes, especially near the nest.
RANGE IN OUR REGION: Migrates along the Appalachian ridges and the Atlantic coastline.
HABITAT: Large cliffs and bluffs near water.

Although the peregrine does not winter with us, this most spectacular bird migrates through our region toward early winter. The intense international interest in the endangered falcon, coupled with the fact that it is readily observable at predictable times and places in our region, calls for its inclusion in this book. Arctic-nesting peregrines migrate southward along the eastern Appalachian ridges, where they may be seen at strategic locations such as Hawk Mountain, Pennsylvania. Coastal "funneling points" such as Cape May, New Jersey, Assateague Island in Maryland and Virginia, and Pea Island and Ocracoke, North Carolina, provide the best lookouts, however. Dedicated naturalists make numerous sightings each autumn at the inland and coastal vantage points.

The peregrine is by tradition the hunting falcon of royalty. Known to exceed 200 mph in a dive (some estimates place the maximum speed at closer to 300 mph), it is the world's fastest bird—for that matter,

♂   ♀

the fastest living creature. The grace and power of its flight beggar description. Beside the peregrine, other birds flop and wallow clumsily through the air.

Technically, only the female is termed a falcon, the smaller male being the tiercel. The differences in color and size are just great enough to be distinguishable when the sexes are seen together. In flight, the peregrine appears somewhat larger than a crow, and the long pointed wings span more than three feet. The species has sixteen races distributed worldwide, the race *anatum* (from the Latin *anas*, meaning duck; hence, "duck hawk") hunting the North American skies.

The duck hawk lives by taking other birds on the wing. It kills with a bone-shattering strike at blinding speed, then alights to mantle the kill and eat. Its exceptional proficiency as a predator enables it to take prey at will. The peregrine sallies forth when hungry, returning in minutes with a blue jay or a flicker or a seabird limp in its talons. A mated pair often hunts together, and one tactic involves a lethal double stoop, or attack dive, with the falcon in the lead. If she misses, the tiercel "binds to" the prey a split second later. In the most spectacular coordinated attack, the tiercel sweeps low over a river or marsh while the falcon "waits on" a half mile above. Ducks usually respond to this lionlike hunting tactic by staying close to cover, but the instant the tiercel puts up a nervous mallard, the falcon streaks downward on the victim. She strikes the duck with a closed fist and administers the coup de grace on the ground by breaking the neck with her notched bill. The hunters meet at the kill, but the falcon always dines first, whether she or the tiercel made the strike.

I first saw the peregrine in early November, 1972, at Pea Island National Wildlife Refuge just north of Cape Hatteras, North Carolina. She swooped low through a scudding drizzle and easily overtook a flight of ducks that was barely making headway against a strong wind. Though she could easily have rolled and struck from below, the falcon showed no interest in the ducks. She flashed beneath them as if the head wind did not apply to her, and vanished over a dike. Later I found the wings of two least sandpipers floating near the edge of the same freshwater impoundment, nipped off neatly at the base, falcon-style, and I recalled reading an account of a peregrine knocking several shorebirds from a flock on a single pass.

My first impression was that I had seen a huge swallow; the silhouette and the wing movements were quite swallowlike. I can best convey the image of the peregrine I saw by suggesting that the reader picture in his or her mind a barn swallow (without forked tail) sweeping low over a pond, then enlarge the swallow six or seven times, increase its speed in proportion, and retain its agility.

At present the peregrine perches precariously near the top of the list of rare and endangered North American birds. It was never common, for its territorial requirements and the scarcity of the cliffs it prefers for nesting kept the pairs miles apart; but now the chlorinated hydrocarbon pesticides, notably DDT, Aldrin and Dieldrin, have extirpated this noblest of birds as a breeding species in eastern North America. The disappearance was abrupt and complete. Well into the 1940's peregrines nested on the rocky cliffs along the Hudson, Potomac and Susquehanna rivers. Some even thrived nesting on skyscrapers in major cities and preying on the starlings and pigeons in the concrete canyons. But within five years after the pesticides were introduced, the poisons had worked their way up the food chain to the peregrines, destroying their reproductive ability. By the mid-fifties, the bird was a rarity. In 1964 a scientist retraced a route that in 1940 yielded 275 peregrine eyries in the United States east of the Rockies, and he found not a single active nest.

Today there is reason for hope and for further despair. The poisons are banned by law, and the subarctic nesting populations continue to produce young. Conceivably, birds from the north may someday reoccupy the southern eyries. On the other hand, wealthy falconers, many from the oil-rich Middle East, are paying immense sums for North American peregrines and, according to the U.S. Fish and Wildlife Service, organized crime is coordinating their procurement. The outcome depends upon vigorous protection and public concern. The extent of the problem is indicated by the case of a California eyrie from which nestlings were stolen in 1973 despite a round-the-clock watch by friends of the peregrine.

The pesticide problem is international in scope. DDT is used intensively in South America, where the arctic-nesting peregrines winter, and scientists expect that this contamination will soon be reflected in reproductive failures in the northern populations. Ironically, these pesticides are manufactured in the United States and, although they are no longer used here, they are freely exported. Somehow our federal sages have concluded that we are doing our Latin friends a favor by selling them poisons too noxious for use in our own environment.

MERLIN OR PIGEON HAWK
Falco columbarius

FIELD MARKS: A small falcon with long, pointed wings. The male is slate gray above, the slightly larger female brownish. The breasts of both sexes are streaked with brown, and there are wide bands in the tails. Juveniles resemble the adult female but have light edgings on the contour feathers of the back and on the wing coverts. All plumages lack the dark facial markings of the peregrine and the kestrel.
LENGTH: 12 inches.
WINGSPAN: 24 inches.
VOICE: A series of short CAKs signaling alarm; occasional high-pitched screeching calls. The voice is not loud.
RANGE IN OUR REGION: Migrates southward along coastline and mountain ridges in fall.
HABITAT: Hunts open spaces, wood margins, marshes and maritime shrub zones while migrating through our region.

The merlin, like the peregrine, does not winter with us, but its migrations take it through our region as late as early winter.

The pigeon hawk derives its common and scientific name from a similarity, seen better perhaps by other observers than by me, to a pigeon in flight. Watching this falcon dive and sprint after flickers at Cape May, New Jersey, on autumn migration, I see a grace and aerobatic mastery no pigeon will ever show. The hunting technique consists of a downward launch from a high perch and a swift exploratory pass through a grove or along a wood margin, followed by a high-speed chase. If the quarry, usually a small bird, makes cover, the pigeon hawk swoops skyward, turns watchfully and dives again in an unexpected direction. The smaller birds in the vicinity of a hunting merlin nervously jockey for cover, and frequently a sparrow who has entered a neighbor's sanctuary is ejected. From this confusion the pigeon hawk can readily snatch a victim.

With the flickers at Cape May, the merlins were probably just playing, for of the dozens of chases I watched with the hunter on the very tail of the prey, none ended in a kill. Bill Clark, who directs the Cape May Bird Observatory, explained that the overwhelming majority of the merlins migrating through Cape May are birds born the previous spring. The young hunters spend much of their time honing their skills in aerial games with other birds. I have seen a young merlin playfully attack an adult peregrine. The great majority of pigeon hawks seen along the coast of our region in autumn wear the brown plumage of juveniles and desport themselves en route in a nearly endless frolic. The adults ply their inland migratory routes along the eastern Appalachian ridges in a more businesslike manner.

The term "merlin" originated in heraldic falconry as the reference for the female. The male was called the "jack." The species was flown as a hunting falcon by northern Asians from perhaps the very birth of falconry four thousand years ago. In feudal Europe the merlin became the favored hawk of royal and noble ladies; Mary Queen of Scots enlivened her days as a prisoner by flying merlins against larks.

Columbarius (from the Latin *columba*, pigeon) breeds in the palearctic forests and tundras and in the boreal forests of North America. It was probably never a "common" bird and has not, at least since the last glaciation, bred in our region. Yet as the northern part of the continent empties the great surpluses of its breeding season along our coastline, we have ample opportunity to see this compact little falcon arrowing in pursuit of smaller birds. An October weekend at Assateague or Pea Island or Huntington Beach with the field glasses ready and the spirit synchronized with the continent's autumnal pulse should yield a merlin sighting.

Woodpeckers *(Order Piciformes)*

PILEATED WOODPECKER
Dryocopus pileatus

FIELD MARKS: A very large woodpecker—as large as a crow. The back and underparts are principally black. A broad white stripe runs from the base of the bill to the rear of the head and down the sides of the neck. A crest slopes upward from the bill, peaking above the rear of the head. The male's crest is entirely red, as are his moustachelike markings. The female lacks the red moustache, and only the rear half of her crest is red. White shows beneath the wings in flight.
LENGTH: 15 inches.
VOICE: A series of wild, loud KUKs similar to the flicker's but slower and softer toward the end.
RANGE IN OUR REGION: Can be found in some localities in all seasons throughout the Carolinas and nearby states.
HABITAT: Mature deciduous and mixed forests in large tracts.

Size is this woodpecker's most impressive feature. Because it is uncommon, we see the pileated infrequently, and each sighting is memorable. Even the seasoned observer must adjust to the idea of a woodpecker the size of a crow.

One January day in Orange County, North Carolina, I had an opportunity to make the often-used comparison firsthand. I saw three birds that looked like crows flying at treetop height across an open field. All were large, black and of equal size. The rearward two were

harassing the lead bird with noisy but cautious attacks. I had never seen crows attack one another, and I began to watch carefully. I noticed that the forward bird, flying on an unperturbed course, had an irregular wingbeat. Then the low sun flashed in the white under its wings, and I knew it was a pileated. The flight pattern and wing markings, rather than the size, distinguished the woodpecker from the crows.

The "logcock," as Yankee woodsmen know him, resembles the nearly extinct ivory-billed, an even larger woodpecker. It was once possible to confuse the two in the southeastern United States, but now only the pileated remains. Logging and the draining of the swamps eliminated the ivorybill. The more versatile pileated survived the destruction of forests in the nineteenth century by retreating to small enclaves in the uplands. Even there, the pileated was shot for food by market hunters and persecuted to near extinction. It somehow lived through this unenlightened period, an environmental dark age from which the continent has never fully recovered. Widespread reforestation and wildlife protection are now helping the pileated increase its numbers.

Today the "stump breaker" can be heard hammering and calling in our wilder wooded tracts. It dwells occasionally in stable landscapes of older residential areas. The photograph above was made at Christmastime in 1975 along the Potomac River within five miles of the city limits of Washington, D.C.

The feeding excavations of the pileated are distinctive rectangular wedges as long as three feet from top to bottom, chiseled into decaying wood. The bird feeds principally on black carpenter ants and on beetle larvae exposed by its relentless digging. Chips the size of matchbooks may litter the ground beneath the great woodsman's works. The entrance to the nesting and roosting cavity is a circular hole three inches across.

RED-COCKADED WOODPECKER
Dendrocopos borealis

FIELD MARKS: The "ladder" of alternating black and white bands covers the back as well as the wings. Large white cheek patches include the eye. At the base of the black cap, toward the rear of the head, the male may have small, bright red cockades. The cockades are normally retracted and are not visible. They are absent in the female. Otherwise, the sexes are indistinguishable.
LENGTH: 8 inches.
VOICE: Squeaks and rapid twitters.
RANGE IN OUR REGION: Winters and nests locally in longleaf, slash and pond pine forests of the Carolinas, Georgia and the Gulf states.
HABITAT: Open pine woods, preferably mature longleaf pines.

The red-cockaded woodpecker is on the U.S. Fish and Wildlife Service's official list of rare and endangered species. The bird is a highly specialized dweller who is limited to the longleaf pine stands of the sandhills section of our region. Clear-cutting and other destructive logging practices have reduced the mature longleaf pine habitat to a mere remnant of its original million-acre grandeur and have nearly extirpated the red-cockaded woodpecker in the process. Perhaps no more than three thousand individuals remain.

The "cockade" is the only bird in the world that drills into living wood to excavate its nesting and roosting cavities. The excavations of this woodpecker are clearly distinguishable from those of any other by the fact that the tree is very much alive and healthy and by the circle of bark removed from around the entrance. The cockade wounds the tree in the vicinity of the hole so that sap weeps downward, giving the appearance

that the trunk is glazed with sugar. Trees bearing older excavations appear to have been whitewashed. The oozing sap provides an effective deterrent to snakes who would otherwise climb the tree and eat the eggs, the young and possibly the adults.

Procurement of food is apparently a problem, because the two parents need the help of additional adults to feed the young. A professional ornithologist who has studied the red-cockaded woodpecker's nesting habits in North Carolina observed that three adults are needed to raise one young, four to raise two, etc. A "family" group of from three to seven birds lives together in all seasons on a territory of approximately one square mile. Toward the center of the territory, they select a group of longleaf pines in which to excavate their living quarters. They rotate the use of these dens between nesting and roosting so that a given cavity is not used for nesting two years in succession. A few vacant cavities are always available for use by other birds and animals.

The longleaf pine habitat is a fire-dependent community. Naturally-caused fires sweep through these forests periodically and kill the deciduous trees, which would otherwise eventually replace the pines. The longleaf pines, protected by an insulating sheath of bark, are fire-resistant. Soon after a longleaf dies, however, the bark loosens and falls, leaving the tree to be consumed by the next fire. Therefore deadwood, which houses other woodpeckers in other habitats, is an uncommon and unstable nesting shelter in the longleaf pines.

Because of the slow rate of growth and the hardness of the wood of the longleaf pines, the cockade must labor as long as five years to mine a cavity suitable for roosting or nesting. If the excavated trees are destroyed, the red-cockaded woodpeckers can not replace their shelters in a few hours as can woodpeckers in other habitats. Homeless cockades usually fall prey to owls within the first few nights after their roosting cavities are destroyed.

The natural consequence of clear-cutting a stand of longleaf pines that contains excavated trees is the elimination of the red-cockaded woodpecker colony. In addition, all other cavity-nesting birds in the habitat (bluebirds, crested flycatchers, chickadees and all other woodpeckers, to name a few) as well as flying squirrels, bees and many other life forms depend on the cockade's excavations for shelter. On the Fort Bragg Military Reservation in North Carolina, a major cockade stronghold on which clear-cutting is banned and controlled burning is practiced, the adoption of enlightened forestry practices holds promise of reducing the threat of extinction. If we are unable to save the red-cockaded woodpecker, the character of an entire habitat will be demeaned, for this single species underpins the life system there.

Perching Birds *(Order Passeriformes)*

FAMILY CORVIDAE

COMMON RAVEN
Corvus corax

FIELD MARKS: This is the largest all-black bird in our region except for the black vulture. The shaggy throat feathers, seen only at close range, and the long, heavy bill are reliable identifiers. In flight, the tail is wedge-shaped. The sexes are indistinguishable.
LENGTH: 21 to 27 inches.
WINGSPAN: 50 to 54 inches.
VOICE: A hoarse CROAK. Numerous musical conversational notes are given while feeding.
RANGE IN OUR REGION: Confined to higher mountain elevations in the southern Appalachians from Virginia to Georgia.
HABITAT: In our region, rugged mountainous highlands. Elsewhere, deserts, seacoasts, forests, from the tropics to the arctic.

In flight, the raven's tail appears distinctly wedge-shaped in contrast with the rounded tail of the common crow. The deep, labored wingbeats are crowlike, but unlike the crow, the raven frequently soars and glides. Playing in the mountain air currents, the raven exhibits aerobatic mastery rivaling that of the hawks and eagles. At close range the raven is seen to be a massive bird almost as large as the black vulture and twice the size of the crow. The long, stiff throat feathers give a shaggy appearance during relaxed moments. The stout, four-inch beak arches like a "Roman nose."

The raven's association with man is steeped in legend, including the belief that disaster is foretold when the bird's shadow crosses the path of a bride. For centuries the British feared their empire might fall if the ravens ever left the Tower of London.

The range of the raven includes all continents except South America, Australia and Antarctica. The world's largest crow, it hunts young seals and seabirds within the Arctic Circle and follows polar bears and wolves

for the leftovers of their kills. It searches the Himalayas for food of many types and scavenges carrion along rivers and coastlines in western North America. Once common on the Great Plains, where it fed on the carcasses of buffalo, the raven retreated to the western mountains and to the northern forests before the onslaught of civilization. In our region the great sable corvid is rare and localized in the remote Appalachian highlands, where it nests on sheer rocky ledges and soars like a hawk in the mountain updrafts.

I have seen the raven soaring near the summit of Mt. Pisgah in North Carolina and have heard its croak on the winds of Mt. Mitchell. Any mountain outing in the North Carolina or Georgia highlands presents the possibility of a sighting. The most reliable location that I know of for encountering the raven is in the Jefferson National Forest near Mountain Lake, Virginia. There is an elegant old resort hotel there, and a score or so of ravens make daily visits to rummage in the hotel's garbage dump. Unfortunately the refuse sometimes contains rat poison, from which a raven died in the summer of 1974 in spite of a veterinarian's best efforts. I helped handle the stricken bird while it was being treated and will never forget how surprisingly large and strong it was.

Descriptions of the raven's voice vary in unkindness from the poet's apocryphal "Nevermore" to L. A. Hausman's "loud, hoarse, dismal, uncouth, prolonged croak, KRAAUUK or KRUUUCK." The croak issued in flight is in fact unmusical, though evocative, especially when borne from a distance on mountain winds. The feeding conversation, however, such as I have often heard at Mountain Lake, offers an incredible range of tones and timbres, most of which are quite musical and pleasing to hear. The melodic gurgles, sighs and whistles pour forth in long passages and present a tonal range and repertoire greater, I believe, than those of the mockingbird.

How the Photographs Were Taken

My photographs were all made with a Nikon 35 mm camera as were those of contributing photographers, unless otherwise noted. My film was Ektachrome in all cases except for the photographs of the sharp-shinned hawk, the Cooper's hawk and the bittern, on which I used Kodachrome 64. Natural light was used when no reference is made to lighting. I have noted the location of photographs made outside Orange County, N.C., where I live. All the photographs were taken between 1969 and 1976.

P. ii.   This photograph depicts birds assembled in my yard in Orange County, N.C., during a snowstorm. The picture was taken from my dining room window with a 50 mm lens, f5.6, 1/60.

P. iv.   The cedar waxwings let me approach to within thirty feet with a 500 mm Vivitar lens, f6.3, 1/250.

P. v.   The red-shouldered hawk permitted me this shot from an automobile in Chatham County, N.C. Nikon 500 mm lens, f8, 1/500.

P. 3.   This flicker permitted me to approach to within thirty feet. I steadied the camera on a unipod, using the Nikon 500 mm lens, f8, 1/250.

P. 5.   The red-bellied woodpecker was descending to a suet cake tacked to a tree ten feet in front of a blind. Nikon 200 mm lens, f8, strobe light.

P. 6.   The hairy woodpecker was photographed at the same setup as the red-bellied, p. 5.

P. 7.   The downy was also photographed at the same setup as the red-bellied, p. 5.

P. 8.   This blue jay came to a feeder six feet in front of a blind. Nikon 200 mm lens (with Micro lens M-ring), f11, strobe light.

P. 9.   Two blue jays simultaneously hammer at sunflower seeds outside my window during a snowstorm. I used a 50 mm lens, f5.6, 1/60.

P. 10.   The chickadee was lit by a strobe through a window near a feeder at Hawk Mountain, Pa. Nikon 200 mm lens, f8.

P. 11.   The Carolina chickadee was photographed from a blind ten feet from a suet cake. Nikon 80–200 mm zoom, f11, strobe light.

P. 12.   Light from a strobe matched the ambient light on the titmouse ten feet from a blind near a feeder. Nikon 80–200 mm zoom, f11.

P. 13.   The white-breasted nuthatch was photographed at the same setup as the Carolina chickadee, p. 11.

P. 14.   Ed Burroughs took this excellent photograph of a red-breasted nuthatch near a feeder from the bedroom window of his home in Eden, N.C. Nikon 200 mm lens, strobe light.

P. 15.   The photograph of the brown-headed nuthatch was made from a portable blind I placed ten feet from a feeding station in a friend's yard near Durham, N.C. Nikon 80–200 mm zoom lens, f8, 1/250.

P. 16.   The Carolina wren came to a feeder six feet outside my dining room window. Nikon 200 mm lens, f11, strobe light.

P. 17.   I photographed the mockingbird from forty feet in Coker Arboretum in Chapel Hill, N.C., using a hand-held Nikon 80–200 mm zoom lens, f5.6, strobe light.

P. 18.   The bluebird lit on a *Verbascum* seedpod outside a blind from which I was photographing another bird's nest. Nikon 80–200 mm zoom lens, f5.6, strobe light.

P. 19.   At Bombay Hook National Wildlife Refuge, Del., I swished this ruby-crowned kinglet to within thirty feet and caught his crest raised in irritation. Nikon 500 mm lens, f8, 1/250.

P. 21.   The starling came to eat before a ground-level blind in which I lay prone. Nikon 80–200 mm zoom lens, f8, strobe light.

P. 22. A mixture of peanut butter, cornmeal and bacon fat attracted the yellow-rumped warbler to a friend's window feeder. Provided I made no movement, the bird made feeding visits even with the window open and me eight feet away in the room. Nikon 80–200 mm zoom lens, f8, strobe light, shutter at 1/15 to register background on a cloudy day.

P. 23. The same setup used for the yellow-rumped warbler, p. 22, produced this picture of a pine warbler.

P. 24. The English sparrow visited a feeding station before a ground-level blind. Nikon 80–200 mm zoom lens, f8, strobe light.

P. 25. This head portrait was made of a hand-held bird. Nikon 55 mm lens, f8, 1/250.

P. 26. The cardinal was photographed from a ground-level blind. Nikon 80–200 mm lens, f8, strobe light.

P. 27. During a snowstorm, this pair of cardinals waited above a feeder outside my bedroom window. Nikon 200 mm lens, f5.6, 1/30.

P. 28. The male evening grosbeak paused in the top of a blue spruce outside my living room window. Nikon 200 mm lens, f5.6 1/500.

P. 29. The female evening grosbeak was among a flock feeding at a friend's feeder. I gently opened a sliding glass door and shot with natural light at f5.6, 1/125.

P. 30. The male purple finch rested between feedings on a limb near the feeder. I built a blind at a corner of my porch which gave me a level vantage. Nikon 80–200 mm zoom lens, f8, strobe light. The finches feeding on the ground were shot from a ground-level blind. Nikon 80–200 mm lens, f8, strobe light.

P. 31. The male house finch was photographed in the setting described for the finches on p. 30.

P. 32. Pine siskins at a feeding station in the N.C. Botanical Garden at Chapel Hill permitted me to approach to within twenty feet. Nikon 200 mm lens, f5.6, 1/250.

P. 33. The blind on my porch yielded this picture of a winter goldfinch. Nikon 80–200 mm zoom lens, f8, strobe light.

P. 34. The goldfinches tolerated me as close as twenty-five feet as they fed on the thistle heads in late summer sunlight. I used a unipod to steady the Vivitar 500 mm lens, f6.3, 1/250.

P. 35. The male towhee was photographed from a ground-level blind, the female through an open window. Strobe lighting was used for both. Nikon 80–200 mm zoom lens, f8.

P. 36. The junco was shot from my porch blind. Nikon 80–200 mm zoom lens, f8, strobe light.

P. 37. I photographed the chipping sparrow through the dining room window during a snowstorm. Nikon 200 mm lens, f5.6, 1/60.

P. 38. The field sparrow approached a feeder on a friend's balcony. Vivitar 500 mm lens (with a Nikon M-ring), f6.3, 1/250 from twenty-five feet.

P. 39. The blind on my porch produced the white-throat's picture. Nikon 80–200 mm zoom, f5.6, 1/250.

P. 40. The fox sparrow fed seven feet in front of my ground-level blind. Nikon 80–200 mm zoom lens, f8, strobe light.

P. 41. A window feeder at my home drew the song sparrow, whom I photographed through the glass. Nikon 200 mm lens, f8, strobe light.

P. 43. The great blue heron took flight as I crept over a dike at Chincoteague National Wildlife Refuge, Va. Nikon 80–200 mm zoom lens, f5.6, 1/500.

P. 45. A friend released this pair of wild turkeys who had been used as breeding stock in captivity. Nikon 80–200 mm zoom lens, f5.6, 1/250.

P. 47. I confess. This is a stuffed bird lent to me by Dwayne Raver, editor of *Wildlife in North Carolina*. The taxidermy, however, is quite realistic and the portrait accurately portrays the grouse. Nikon 80–200 mm zoom lens, f5.6, 1/125.

129 / *How the Photographs Were Taken*

P. 47. I photographed the quail from a car, which got stuck, as the covey crossed a road at the Chincoteague National Wildlife Refuge, Va. Nikon 500 mm lens, f8, 1/250.

P. 49. The great blue heron stood near an alligator in the Everglades. The bird permitted me to approach to within seventy-five feet. Nikon 500 mm lens, f8, 1/500.

P. 50. The black-crowned night heron obliged in a marsh within the town limits of Chincoteague, Va. I approached on foot to within fifty feet. Nikon 500 mm lens, f8, 1/250.

P. 51. The bittern suffered me to aim a Nikon 200–600 mm zoom lens (f11, 1/250) at him (or her) after a half-hour stalk at the edge of a marsh near Smyrna, Del.

P. 52. The motor drive on my Nikon F–2 (f8, 1/500) enabled me to get these two shots as the killdeer made a pass.

P. 54. Joel Arrington used a Leica with a Kilfit 90 mm lens to photograph this nesting woodcock, who permitted close approach.

P.55 I built a blind against a roadbank near a moist low area in a pasture on Bob Nutter's farm in Orange County, N.C. The snipe fed cautiously in the mud, never coming closer than fifty feet from the blind. Nikon 500 mm lens.

P. 56. This relatively tame pigeon permitted me to shoot from thirty feet. Nikon 200 mm lens, f8, 1/250.

P. 57. The mourning dove was photographed from a ground-level blind in Chapel Hill, N.C. Nikon 80–200 mm zoom lens, f8, strobe light.

P. 59. Kingfishers are among the wariest of birds, and attracting them to a feeding situation seems nearly impossible. This belted kingfisher, perched atop a sign at Chincoteague National Wildlife Refuge, permitted me to approach to within seventy feet. Nikon 500 mm lens, f8, 1/60.

P. 60. This red-headed woodpecker was photographed from a sidewalk in Chapel Hill, N.C., with a hand-held 200 mm Nikon lens, f8, 1/250. Urban birds are sometimes quite tame.

P. 61. I captured this photograph of the yellow-bellied sapsucker while on a walk in the Coker Arboretum, Chapel Hill, N.C. Hand-held Vivitar 500 mm lens, f6.3, 1/250.

P. 63. This Eastern phoebe permitted close approach to one of her favorite feeding perches. Hand-held Nikon 500 mm lens, f8, 1/250.

P. 64. The horned lark was photographed at Chincoteague, Va., from a concealed position on the ground. Nikon 500 mm lens, f8, 1/250.

P. 65. I tried for six years to get a portrait of the exceptionally wary common crow before finding a population of rather tame individuals near a ranger station in the Everglades National Park, Fla., in January, 1976. Nikon 500 mm lens, 1/500.

P. 66. I happened to have a camera in my car when I saw this crow harassing the red-tailed hawk. I won no driving safety awards in jumping from my still-moving vehicle to get this photograph with a Nikon 200 mm lens at f5.6, 1/500.

P. 67. It was a stroke of luck to catch this flying fish crow in sharp focus with a hand-held Vivitar 500 mm lens in a situation which clearly includes its favored habitat. Chincoteague, Va., f6.3, 1/500.

P. 68. This brown creeper was probably drawn more from curiosity than hunger to a tree on which other birds were feeding on a mixture of cornmeal, bacon fat and peanut butter. It did not feed. "Luck" usually works against the photographer of birds, for so many factors must conspire favorably. As the creeper made this fortuitous visit and passed through the field of vision of my camera four feet away, I happened to have my finger on the release button. The bird was not visible through the camera for more than a second, and I consider this a "lucky shot" indeed. Nikon 80–200 mm zoom lens, f8, strobe light.

P. 69. The winter wren is an exceptionally wary bird

and one that I have never known to visit a feeding situation. This picture was taken in the wild near College Park, Md., as the bird flitted among the roots of trees exposed along the bank of a stream. Hand-held Vivitar 500 mm lens, f6.3, 1/250.

P. 70. The brown thrasher is also notably camera shy. This individual took an exposed position to harass a cat in my yard in Carrboro, N.C. Nikon 500 mm lens, f8, 1/250.

P. 71. A blustering March wind ruffled the breast of this robin in Coker Arboretum, Chapel Hill, N.C., as I focused with the Vivitar 500 mm lens, f6.3, 1/250.

P. 72. As I waited in a concealed position for some horned larks at Chincoteague, Va., this hermit thrush left its characteristic wetland hardwood habitat to feed in the open. Nikon 200–600 mm zoom lens, f11, 1/250.

P. 73. At Huntington Beach, S.C., Stanley Alford caught this golden-crowned in a shrub just as it took flight. He had stalked and "swished" the bird for thirty minutes. Nikon 500 mm lens, 1/500.

P. 74. I photographed this water pipit at twelve thousand feet in the Bridger Wilderness, Wy. Hand-held Nikon 500 mm lens, f8, 1/500.

P. 75. I caught this feeding group of cedar waxwings in a tree across from the Carolina Inn in Chapel Hill, N.C. They permitted a close approach with a hand-held Nikon 500 mm lens, f8, 1/250.

P. 76. Stanley Alford photographed this palm warbler after a diligent stalk at Huntington Beach State Park, S.C. Hand-held 500 mm lens.

P. 77. This common yellowthroat popped to the surface of a briar patch to protest my swishing. I used a strobe and 500 mm hand-held Nikon lens. The picture was made in an unflooded lake bed above the B. Everett Jordan Dam on the New Hope River, Chatham County, N.C.

P. 79. This slightly cat-chewed eastern meadowlark was brought to me by a neighbor. It posed briefly on a grass tussock, recuperated for two weeks in a cage, and was released. Nikon 80–200 mm zoom lens, f8, 1/250.

P. 80. I spent several hours on two different occasions on the balcony of a friend's home overlooking a lake. This male red-winged blackbird came into sharp focus through my 500 mm lens (f6.3, 1/500) as he made a display pass near one of his nesting mates. Focusing on moving targets with long lenses is extremely difficult because of the narrow depth of field. This shot is the product of five rolls of film.

P. 81. The rusty blackbird was photographed along a stream in Orange County, N.C. The bird permitted me to approach to within forty feet. Hand-held Nikon 500 mm lens, f8, 1/250.

P. 83. The common grackle was photographed at the edge of my garden in Carrboro, N.C., with a Nikon 500 mm lens, f8, 1/500.

P. 84. The savannah sparrow permitted me to approach to within thirty feet in its short-grassed habitat at Chincoteague, Va. Nikon 500 mm lens from an automobile.

P. 85. The grasshopper sparrow is in his open field habitat near College Park, Md. The bird lit on the barbed wire thirty-five feet away and paused for a moment. The 500 mm lens was hand-held at f6.3 and 1/500.

P. 86. This singing male white-crowned sparrow responded to my swishing by defiantly perching atop a scrub pine in Yosemite National Park, Cal. The hand-held Nikon 500 mm lens (f8, 1/500) captured, at eight thousand feet elevation, the bright sunlight reflected in the bird's erect crest.

P. 87. This fine photograph of a swamp sparrow was made by Stanley Alford after a long stalk and much swishing. It was taken at B. Everett Jordan Dam, Chatham County, N.C., with a Nikon 500 mm lens.

P. 89. Shortly after this picture was made, the horned

131 / *How the Photographs Were Taken*

owl made a series of passes at me but never actually struck. I was too close to a newly fledged chick of hers (his). To get this picture in the dim light of sunset filtering into the winter woods, I sat on the ground, propped the long barrel of the Vivitar 500 mm lens on my knees, and shot at f6.3 and 1/60.

P. 91.   The turkey vulture was photographed through a hand-held 500 mm lens (f8, 1/500) as the bird made a pass over a carcass near which I was hidden in Orange County, N.C.

P. 92.   This turkey vulture waited near a carcass for its turn to feed. Nikon 500 mm lens, f8, 1/250.

P. 93.   The black vulture shows the white patches under its wings as it departs from its perch in a power trestle in Orange County, N.C. Hand-held Nikon 500 mm lens, f8, 1/500.

P. 94.   This black vulture pretended not to notice as I "stalked" through the dry leaves of a woods through which a power line ran in Orange County, N.C. I took the picture from about a hundred feet with the Nikon 500 mm lens, f8, 1/500.

P. 95.   This migrating Cooper's hawk was photographed at Hawk Mountain, Pa. On one trip I spent several days at this unbelievably fruitful raptor migration site using a Nikon 200–600 mm zoom lens and a motor-driven Nikon camera. The trip yielded portraits of the Cooper's and sharp-shinned hawks taken from comparable angles and showing the difference in tail shapes.

P. 97.   The sharp-shinned was photographed at the same setup as the Cooper's, p. 95.

P. 98.   This female marsh hawk was photographed at Chincoteague, Va., as she reversed her flight at the end of a low pass. Hand-held 500 mm lens, f8, 1/500.

P. 100.   A red-tailed frequently used a tulip tree along my driveway as a hunting perch. This picture was taken from a moving automobile, since the bird always flew instantly if a car even slowed down.

Vivitar 500 mm lens, f6.3, at 1/1000 of a second. Compensation was made in processing for a two-stop underexposure.

P. 102.   The red-shouldered hawk was photographed as it passed, unconcerned, overhead in the Everglades National Park, Fla. Nikon 500 mm lens, f8, 1/500.

P. 103.   This male sparrow hawk is a captive bird belonging to Dr. Helmut Mueller of UNC, Chapel Hill. I took the pictures in his laboratory.

P. 104.   This photograph of the female sparrow hawk was also taken at Dr. Mueller's laboratory at UNC.

P. 105.   A friend permitted me to photograph his pet screech owl in a dogwood tree in his front yard in Chapel Hill, N.C. Sunset light, Nikon 80–200 mm zoom lens, f5.6, 1/250.

P. 107.   This immature great horned owl had been hand-raised. It permitted my close approach with the Nikon 500 mm lens (f8, 1/250) at Hawk Mountain, Pa. A few minutes later it "attacked" a doughnut left by a visitor.

P. 108.   I photographed these great horned owl chicks (the offspring of the bird shown on p. 89) about a week after they fledged. I spotted them roosting and they permitted me to approach to within a hundred feet. Vivitar 500 mm lens, f6.3, 1/250.

P. 109.   The barred owl here is a completely wild bird who had just left her nest and regarded me resentfully from a nearby tree in Umstead Park, Chapel Hill, N.C. Vivitar 500 mm lens, f6.3, 1/60. The camera was rested against a tree.

P. 111.   The loggerhead shrike is normally a wary bird, but this one permitted my close approach in an automobile in Orange County, N.C. Nikon 500 mm lens, f8, 1/250.

P. 113.   I spotted this immature peregrine resting in an open tidal flat on Ocracoke Island, N.C., in November, 1974. There was no cover to utilize in stalking the youngster, so I simply approached on foot, very slowly, stopping frequently to reduce the apparent threat. At a hundred yards it took flight. I took a series of pictures with the motor-driven Nikon and 500 mm lens at 1/500.

P. 115. This is a captive bald eagle, photographed in a flight cage at the National Wildlife Research Station, Patuxent, Md. Nikon 80–200 mm zoom lens, f5.6, 1/250.

P. 117. Crossing the Delaware River north of Philadelphia, Pa., I saw this osprey over the water. It obligingly appeared overhead as I pulled off the road at the end of the bridge. Nikon 500 mm lens, f8, 1/500.

P. 119. This pair of peregrines participates in a U.S. Fish and Wildlife Service effort to get the rare birds to breed in captivity. The staff of the Patuxent Wildlife Research Center in Maryland graciously consented to have me photograph the birds. Nikon 80–200 mm zoom lens, f8, 1/250.

P. 121. This young merlin was captured for banding at Cape May Point, N.J. Nikon 55 mm macro lens, f8, 1/60.

P. 123. Near MacLean, Va., a pileated woodpecker, normally wary, permitted me to stalk to within sixty feet with the Nikon 500 mm lens. The overcast day obliged me to make a 1/8 second exposure. The picture is sharp only because I was able to anchor the camera in the crotch of a tree and catch the bird motionless.

P. 125. Jay Carter of Southern Pines, N.C., staked me out at a cockade's nest in Weymouth Woods. Vivitar 500 mm lens, f6.3, 1/250.

P. 127. I photographed the common raven passing over my head at Mountain Lake, Va. This raven shows its characteristic V-shaped tail. Vivitar 500 mm lens, f6.3, 1/500 of a second.

Index

(Boldface figures indicate illustrated descriptions of the birds)

This book is set in 10 on 13 Palatino
Book design by Virginia Ingram
Photographs by the author
Drawings by Bruce Tucker
Composition by Heritage Printers, Inc.,
Charlotte, North Carolina
Printing by Lebanon Valley Offset Company, Inc.
Annville, Pennsylvania
on Warren's Lustro Offset Enamel Dull, White, 80-lb.
The binding is Columbia's Bayside BVC–4881
by Optic Bindery, Baltimore, Maryland
Endpapers are Strathmore Grandee 80-lb. text